CW01158045

EMINENT VICTORIANS
ON AMERICAN DEMOCRACY

EMINENT VICTORIANS ON AMERICAN DEMOCRACY

THE VIEW FROM ALBION

FRANK PROCHASKA

OXFORD
UNIVERSITY PRESS

OXFORD
UNIVERSITY PRESS

Great Clarendon Street, Oxford OX2 6DP

Oxford University Press is a department of the University of Oxford.
It furthers the University's objective of excellence in research, scholarship,
and education by publishing worldwide in

Oxford New York

Auckland Cape Town Dar es Salaam Hong Kong Karachi
Kuala Lumpur Madrid Melbourne Mexico City Nairobi
New Delhi Shanghai Taipei Toronto

With offices in

Argentina Austria Brazil Chile Czech Republic France Greece
Guatemala Hungary Italy Japan Poland Portugal Singapore
South Korea Switzerland Thailand Turkey Ukraine Vietnam

Oxford is a registered trade mark of Oxford University Press
in the UK and in certain other countries

Published in the United States
by Oxford University Press Inc., New York

© Frank Prochaska 2012

The moral rights of the author have been asserted
Database right Oxford University Press (maker)

Crown copyright material is reproduced under Class Licence
Number C01P0000148 with the permission of OPSI
and the Queen's Printer for Scotland

First published 2012

All rights reserved. No part of this publication may be reproduced,
stored in a retrieval system, or transmitted, in any form or by any means,
without the prior permission in writing of Oxford University Press,
or as expressly permitted by law, or under terms agreed with the appropriate
reprographics rights organization. Enquiries concerning reproduction
outside the scope of the above should be sent to the Rights Department,
Oxford University Press, at the address above

You must not circulate this book in any other binding or cover
and you must impose the same condition on any acquirer

British Library Cataloguing in Publication Data

Data available

Library of Congress Cataloging in Publication Data

Library of Congress Control Number: 2011942648

Typeset by SPI Publisher Services, Pondicherry, India
Printed in Great Britain
on acid-free paper by
MPG Books Group, Bodmin and King's Lynn

ISBN 978–0–19–964061–4

1 3 5 7 9 10 8 6 4 2

Preface

Distance lends perspective. In a period undergoing another impasse in American politics, when rival priesthoods see the Constitution in the light kindled at their particular altars, it is perhaps worth revisiting what leading Victorian thinkers had to say about the most advanced democracy of their day. A great many Britons observed America in the nineteenth century, some on their travels, others from their studies; and a fair number of them play a part in this survey, from Harriet Martineau and Mrs Trollope to A. V. Dicey and William Lecky. But John Stuart Mill, Walter Bagehot, Sir Henry Maine, and James Bryce take precedence here. They have been chosen rather than other protagonists not simply because they were 'Eminent Victorians', to borrow Lytton Strachey's phrase, but because they engaged more seriously in constitutional issues than writers such as Charles Dickens, wrote more extensively on America than scholars such as Lord Acton, and left a critique of the United States government that illuminates its political malaise.

Much opinion of the United States from Europe in the nineteenth century may now come as a shock to Americans, whose pride in their uniqueness rarely warms to analysis from abroad. There have been exceptions, of course, the most notable being Alexis de Tocqueville, who may have been a more acceptable critic because he was French and who shrewdly leavened his reproaches with lashings of praise in *Democracy in America*. Tocqueville's masterwork, which appeared at the dawn of the Victorian age, framed much of the British discussion about American democracy. Mill, Bagehot, Maine, and Bryce all came under its influence, though at different periods from different perspectives and with different responses. Though generally less flattering and speculative than the Frenchman, they were no less incisive. Moreover, they dealt with a host of issues, most importantly the Civil War and its aftermath, which Tocqueville did not live to experience.

While their political opinions varied, the Victorians highlighted in this study agreed about important aspects of American government, among them the failings of its electoral politics and the poor calibre of its leaders. All of them rejected the idea of American 'exceptionalism', which has never appealed to the British, who had a proprietary interest in seeing continuity from the government of the former colonies. To Victorian commentators, the bonds of kinship, law, and language were of great significance; and while they did not see the United States as having a providential destiny, they rallied to an 'Anglo-American exceptionalism', which reflected their sense of a shared history. Constitutional affinities between the two nations, often ignored by Americans, were crucial to their analyses. What distinguishes them from contemporary American commentators was a willingness to examine the US Constitution dispassionately, at a time when it had become a sacred document in America and consequently little subject to critical observation.

The Victorians were part of a new era in the study of British and European politics, in which a fundamental issue was the shifting balance of power from aristocratic to popular government. While all the writers surveyed here engaged in the debate over democracy, they were not all on the side of reform. America was significant to them because it raised universal questions about political behaviour and was seen to anticipate the future of Europe. Apart from their perceptive examination of issues ranging from the US Constitution to its practical application, from the Supreme Court and party enmity, the Victorians made a memorable contribution to what may be seen as the ongoing Anglo-American debate over the origins of democracy. America has changed dramatically since they wrote, yet much of their criticism remains remarkably prescient today, if only because the US government retains so much of its original, eighteenth-century character. This book will have served its purpose if it encourages readers to return to the writings of these exceptional thinkers, whose trenchant commentary on America punctures several modern-day myths.

* * *

This project began life in New Haven and ended in Oxford. I am thus indebted to friends and colleagues on both sides of the Atlantic for this most transatlantic of subjects. As ever, librarians have made my researches congenial, most notably at the Sterling Memorial Library at

Yale, the Bodleian Library in Oxford, and the Library of Somerville College Oxford, which houses a unique collection of the books of John Stuart Mill. My warmest thanks go to John Sainty for his careful reading of the manuscript, and to Geoffrey Shaw, my former student at Yale and now a Rhodes Scholar, who provided a perceptive commentary at a timely moment in the revision process. This is my fifth book with the Oxford University Press, and its expert readers provided valuable observations and criticisms for which I am most grateful. Particular thanks go to Sophie Goldsworthy, Christopher Wheeler, Emma Barber, Jane Robson, and Stephanie Ireland of the OUP, whose good offices brought the book to fruition. Finally, I would like to thank my wife Alice and our children Elizabeth and William for their advice and encouragement. They support me in dedicating the book to a treasured friend, with whom I hope to raise many a glass in the years ahead.

F.P.

Oxford, 2011

Contents

1. Introduction: Transatlantic Attitudes — 1
2. John Stuart Mill: The Tyranny of Conformity — 23
3. Walter Bagehot: The Tyranny of the Constitution — 47
4. Sir Henry Maine: Democracy Denied — 72
5. James Bryce: Anglo-Saxon Democracy — 96
6. Conclusion: Anglo-American Exceptionalism — 122

Notes — 143
Index — 165

To James Sheehan

A great democratic revolution is taking place among us: all see it, but all do not judge it in the same manner. Some consider it a new thing, and taking it for an accident, they still hope to be able to stop it; whereas others judge it irresistible because to them it seems the most continuous, the oldest, and the most permanent fact known in history.

(Alexis de Tocqueville, 1840)

I

Introduction

Transatlantic Attitudes

> Under which of the old tyrannical governments of Europe is every sixth man a Slave, whom his fellow-creatures may buy and sell and torture?
>
> (Sydney Smith, 1820)

> The mariner no more looks to his compass or takes his departure by the sun, than does the lover of liberty think of taking his departure without reference to the constitution of the United States.
>
> (Daniel Webster, 1834)

The United States Constitution, the world's most ancient written Constitution, is a republican substitute for hereditary kingship, and, like kingship, hedged with divinity. Americans treat it like scripture.[1] If the rhetoric of political campaigns and standard schoolbooks are any guide, most US citizens believe, in words attributed to President Coolidge, that 'to live under the American Constitution is the greatest political privilege that was ever accorded to the human race'.[2] Since Washington's presidency, every administration has had dogged critics, but the foundation documents of the nation have remained largely free of censure since the early days of the republic. Few Americans would dispute President Obama's observation at the Naval Academy soon after his election: 'the values and ideas in those documents are not simply words written into aging parchment; they are the bedrock of our liberty and our security'.[3]

It is easy to forget the spirited contest over the Constitution at the time of its adoption in 1787. Even a future President, James Monroe of

Virginia, opposed it. Disputes over the role of the executive, between large and small states, and between North and South over slavery resulted in a document that its opponents predicted would destroy the states as commonwealths, promote foreign wars, lead to aristocratic corruption, and create a despot in the person of the President. Supporters, on the other hand, believed it would mitigate what were thought to be the characteristic dangers of popular government: the violent impulses of the public, mob rule, ill-considered legislation, and an unstable foreign policy.

Various commentators doubted that the new nation would survive given the profound differences of opinion. The battle ensued when it went out to the states for ratification. In the press and the state conventions, the debate largely pitted those who wanted a strong central government against those who preferred a weak league of states. In the process, the divisions created competing factions, the Federalists and the Anti-Federalists, and inspired the *Federalist*, the classic of political thought written in defence of the Constitution. None of the accusations levelled at the Constitution at the time proved decisive. It created neither a tyranny nor triggered a war. But lurking in the background was the persistent issue of party faction, which the Founding Fathers feared would threaten to subvert both individual rights and national interests. James Madison in the *Federalist* had been highly critical of factionalism, whose 'causes' could not be removed but whose 'effects' needed to be controlled.[4] In his farewell address, Washington warned his fellow countrymen of the 'baneful effects of the spirit of party'.[5]

The constitutional debate also engaged the English, who, as colonizers and fellow Anglo-Saxons, felt a sense of ownership in the American government. The political reformers among them, who had supported the colonists in the Revolution, were sympathetic to a resolution of American differences by constitutional means. Others, still stinging from the loss of the colonies, took a more jaundiced view of the proceedings across the Atlantic. In 1788, *The Times* of London thought the principles on which the Constitution had been constructed so clashed with the interests and traditions of the disparate states that producing a lasting harmony between them was highly questionable. 'Speculative politicians', it observed, 'are apt to conclude, that America, like most other nations where a revolution suddenly founded a new Government, will not see a permanent constitution established, without first experiencing much civil contention.'[6]

There was no shortage of civil contention before all thirteen states ratified the Constitution, but once established it served as a domestic peace treaty. It bound Americans to a political settlement with the full grandeur of the law, convincing many of them that they had fulfilled the promise of the Revolution as the most enlightened nation on earth. When the states came on board, the citizenry celebrated with republican parades, which served to disguise the enduring sectional interests and differences. In July 1788, though not every state had yet joined the union, Benjamin Rush, a member of the Pennsylvania Convention that adopted the Federal Constitution, proclaimed: 'Tis done! We have become a nation.' The Constitution, he added, had produced 'such a tide of joy as has seldom been felt in any age or country'.[7]

In 1889, the legal scholar Abbott Lawrence Lowell, later President of Harvard, remarked: 'the Constitution was to us what a king has often been to other nations'.[8] Like a monarch, the US Constitution became a source and symbol of national unity, not simply an instrument of governance.[9] Americans knew from their colonial experience that royal ceremony could be unifying, for as subjects of the Crown they had bowed to their king and demonstrated their allegiance through ritual celebrations of coronations and royal birthdays.[10] In *Popular Government* (1885), the Victorian Sir Henry Maine argued that the United States only became a nation because its people 'once obeyed a king'.[11] But the revolutionaries had demonized George III as a 'tyrant' and the new nation no longer celebrated a family on the throne. As a republic without a monarch or hallowed national symbols, it required substitutes for the ceremonials of royalty. Consequently, Americans, for want of a hereditary king, turned to their founding documents, whose clauses stirred a sense that they were uniquely blessed for not having one.

In the Constitution, Americans produced an instrument of government that served as a powerful ceremonial document around which they could rally as a nation. A transformative moment came in April 1789, when Washington swore the first presidential oath to the Constitution under Article 2. It was the republican substitute for a newly elected Prime Minister 'kissing hands' with the British monarch to form a government. Here was a republican 'invented tradition', like the inauguration itself, which drew heavily on the ceremonial of a British coronation.[12] Ever after, the written Constitution, like an immortal sovereign, bestowed legitimacy, becoming a fixture above and beyond the political process. The Federal government enhanced the significance of the document when it added a Bill of Rights, a further touchstone of America's freedoms, which came into effect in 1791. It was remarkable that such a contested Constitution soon established itself in the public mind as the wellspring of good government, a beacon of freedom, and a foundation stone of American 'exceptionalism'. The timing of its apotheosis has been disputed, though the weight of evidence suggests that it happened quickly.[13] The document liberated the nation from uncertainty, which contributed to its initial success. It established a fixed historical landmark that provided stability, which the public desired after the trauma of the Revolution and the troubled years that followed the peace treaty with Britain. By the end of George Washington's presidency, it was widely seen as blasphemy to doubt its sanctity. Indeed, in his farewell address, Washington declared that the Constitution was the great charter that was 'sacredly obligatory upon all'. It provided 'the unity of government which constitutes you one people.... It is justly so; for it is a main pillar in the edifice of your real independence; the support of your tranquillity at home; your peace abroad; of your safety; of your prosperity; of that very liberty which you so highly prize.'[14]

Despite disturbances in the 1790s and an electoral crisis in 1800–1, it became an article of faith to the competing factions and parties that the Constitution provided a basis of national pride, which was needed urgently in an unstable federation of states jealous of their rights. The framers were well aware of the dangers that might develop with a more malleable Constitution, subject to easy amendment. Given the centrifugal forces in the young republic, would the fragile central state have endured with a more flexible Constitution? Patriotic pride in the timeless nature of the document was thought essential if the Union was, as a nineteenth-century American historian put it, to be 'saved from the consequences of impending anarchy'.[15] As a sovereign instrument of the public will, the Constitution became hallowed, something to be paraded on 4 July to rally the patriots and promote national unity. As Washington observed: 'The name American which belongs to you in your national capacity, must always exalt the just pride of patriotism.'[16]

America, it has been said, lacked the traditional sources of nationhood, so had to locate its national identity elsewhere. 'Union became a synonym for nation.'[17] The formation of the Federal Constitution was a demonstration of the progress of the republic, a momentous step towards creating a distinctive national identity. John Jay remarked that Americans were 'the first people whom heaven has favoured with an opportunity of deliberating upon and choosing the forms of government under which they should live'.[18] As the nation expanded, trade prospered, and the Union endured, there was less and less incentive to question a Constitution that had attained a mythic status. The notion that the document was somehow above politics, not a part of politics, encouraged its consecration. It was, as Madison called it in 1809, 'the cement of the Union', which stirred pride in the nation if not an understanding of government.[19] Along with that other hallowed text, the Declaration of Independence, it provided the wherewithal for Americans to worship their country, and themselves.

The American literature on the United States Constitution after the birth of the republic may seem puzzling to students of politics today. Here was a disputed document that nonetheless soon gained currency among the political classes. Given the ardent patriotism in the republic, the Constitution was seen as the product of 'an assemblage of the gods' and therefore immune to criticism.[20] Indeed, the canonization of the Constitution went hand in hand with canonization of the Founding Fathers themselves, for the document was their most tangible achievement. School textbooks told the story of the nation's birth and the Constitution, like Parson Weems's biography of Washington, without the warts. With the passing years, the patina of age tended to silence irreverent critics.

In a nation searching for a New World identity, the animated debate that marked the Constitutional Convention gave way to the promotion of a distinctive political culture that centred on the contested idea of popular sovereignty.[21] Disputes persisted over the Federal Constitution, not least who counted as 'the people' in the American polity. But there were no successors of the stature of Hamilton or Madison—no updated *Federalist*—to illuminate the practical workings of the US government once it was in motion. In the constitutional commentary a period of complacency set in, which the Federal government encouraged by its success in putting the nation's affairs in order. After all the politicking and dissension during the passage of the Constitution, once it was in place—with a Supreme Court established to interpret it—little thought was given to examining the machinery of government to judge its effectiveness. 'Almost from the start', observed a British scholar, 'it was put into the care of a priesthood, the lawyers, who, from time to time, have opened the Sibylline Book, and told the multitude what was the judgement of the ancestors on situations which it is highly improbable that the ancestors had ever foreseen.'[22]

There were, to be sure, distinguished American commentators on the Constitution in the early decades of the republic, such as the jurists James Kent and Joseph Story; and great 'expounders', such as John Marshall and Daniel Webster. But their writings were more often amplifications of the text or technical interpretations of it as a legal document rather than critical studies of the operation of the presidential system. As the historian Charles Beard remarked in *An Economic Interpretation of the Constitution of the United States* (1913), the great nineteenth-century legal commentaries were 'designed to inculcate the spirit of reverence rather than understanding'.[23] Surprisingly little was written that provided a comprehensive account of the Constitution, though historians exhaustively studied the Revolution and the Founding Fathers.[24] Over time, the study of the Federal Constitution became largely a study of Supreme Court decisions that interpreted the document.[25]

Nor had American historians, as Beard complained, done much to shed a critical light on the Constitution. Few spoke of the document as a compromise necessary to forge the Union and most overlooked its apparent contradictions. Those of the revolutionary generation, such as David Ramsay and Jeremy Belknap, wished to create a national history and lay the foundations of a united people. Consequently, they minimized the internal conflict over the Constitution, preferring to see it as the culminating act of the Revolution that steered the nation towards its providential destiny.[26] Generations of patriotic historians followed in their footsteps, encouraging a nationalistic bias, in which they exalted the Founding Fathers and the Constitution.[27] The most eminent of them in the nineteenth century, the romantic idealist George Bancroft, pronounced that the formation of the US Constitution was

the most cheering act in the political history of mankind.... The sublime achievement was the work of a people led by statesmen of earnestness, perseverance, and public spirit, instructed by the widest experience in the forms of representative government, and warmed by that mutual love which proceeds from ancient connection, harmonious effort in perils, and common aspirations.[28]

In the first century of the republic much of the prevailing American political literature reinforced the theme that the Constitution was a sanctified text and, as such, resistant to the norms of scientific political inquiry. Those who vilified the Constitution in the late 1780s, many of them local politicians, did so because they thought its adoption would be the death knell of states' rights and popular liberties.[29] That the opposition dissipated was a tribute to the document, the eminence of its framers, and the need for a workable union in a world in which the disparate states were individually vulnerable. For their part, constitutional scholars, with the endorsement of American historians, soon came around to the assumption that the equipoise of federal and state governments and the division of power between the executive, legislative, and judicial branches, 'each sovereign in its respective sphere', had achieved perfection or the closest thing to it in the annals of mankind.

The Constitution fulfilled the desire of Americans for order and tranquillity but in the process blinded them to its defects, which were more apparent to foreigners who did not share its benefits. Before the American Anti-Slavery Society formed in 1833, few Americans took the Constitution to task for sanctioning slavery.[30] (It accommodated slavery though the word itself was not mentioned in the text.[31]) Few complained of the difficulty in amending a document that was designed to favour safety and the status quo over action and reform. Few made distinctions between an abstract, idealized Constitution and the practical realities of governance. As long as the document remained above politics it discouraged analysis of American government as it actually functioned. One exception to the Constitutional cult that emerged in the nineteenth century was the journalist and academic Albert Shaw, who remarked in the 1880s, 'the casuists of the Constitution' dealt 'only with the theories, conceptions, and fictions of law'. They had 'no parallel except in the metaphysical theology of the schoolmen'.[32]

In reviewing Alexis de Tocqueville's *Democracy in America*, the British philosopher John Stuart Mill noted that, as 'the state of society becomes more democratic, it is more and more necessary to nourish patriotism by artificial means'.[33] The whole edifice of American government, he added, was built on abstract principles of recent memory. Since the fledgling United States was a political experiment on the fringes of the civilized world, American constitutional writers aimed at nation building not dispassionate analysis. The young Abraham Lincoln contributed to this tradition in a memorable speech in Springfield, Illinois, in 1838,

'The Perpetuation of our Political Institutions'. In priestly language he called 'a reverence for the constitution' the basis of patriotism:

> Let reverence for the laws, be breathed by every American mother, to the lisping babe, that prattles on her lap—let it be taught in schools, in seminaries, and in colleges; let it be written in Primers, spelling books, and in Almanacs;—let it be preached from the pulpit, proclaimed in legislative halls and enforced in the courts. And, in short, let it become the political religion of the nation.[34]

Just as Lincoln desired, politicians and preachers, schools and colleges, proclaimed the words of the Constitution as if at prayer. Meanwhile, officials distributed copies of the founding documents to libraries and public offices across the country, where they were placed on display. The declared purpose, as one promoter remarked in the 1840s, was 'to impress upon Americans a reverential attachment to the Constitution, as in the highest sense the palladium of American liberty'.[35] In a marvel of abstract reasoning, American legal theorists cast a spell over the willing public through their speeches and writings on the Constitution. Such authors had, according to Shaw 'bewitched and bewildered their fellow-countrymen into the belief that our political system is something absolutely apart and not comparable with any other system, nor susceptible of study by the matter-of-fact "observational" methods'.[36]

James Kent, Professor of Law at Columbia, set the tone in his exhaustive *Commentaries on American Law* (1826–30), in which he linked the Constitution to 'national greatness' and the 'general liberties of mankind'. Such sanguine assumptions coloured his discussion of the workings of government. In the flurry of praise, he failed to recognize the tensions and disharmonies created by the competing sovereignties and electoral procedures enshrined in the Constitution. As to slavery, it was an evil 'too deeply rooted, to be speedily eradicated, or even to be discussed without judgment and discretion'. As to the origins of the Constitution, Kent might have been more generous to the British, but in his comparative politics there was only one victor. Britain, he conceded, was 'an asylum of liberty' compared to other European states, but its government was essentially 'feudal', and the House of Commons 'an imperfect organ of the will of the people'.[37]

In his learned *Commentaries on the United States Constitution* (1833), Joseph Story, a Justice of the Supreme Court, was also determined to see the American form of government as unique and exceptional, befitting a new nation that had broken politically with its colonial past.

He set out the document's antecedents and provisions in the hope that students would see it 'as the truest security of the Union, and the only solid basis, on which to rest the private rights, and public liberties, and the substantial prosperity of the people composing the American Republic'. He never doubted that the Founding Fathers had, with consummate skill, created an exceptional polity, 'reared for immortality' with 'the seal of eternity...upon it'.[38]

In his chapter on the origins of the Constitution, Story studiously ignored England, which does not even make the index of his massive study. He conceded that it was the most enlightened of monarchies, but America had created a novel political structure with little reference to Britain. Anxious to create a sense of national unity built out of the Constitution, he concluded that he would be content 'if these Commentaries shall but inspire the rising generation with a more ardent love of their country, an unquenchable thirst for liberty, and a profound reverence for the constitution and the Union'.[39] The language was reminiscent of that often used by patriotic Britons for their monarchy, though the royal family attracted more critics.

Story's friend Daniel Webster, the leading Whig Senator and statesman, speaking in Concord, New Hampshire, in 1834, said the Constitution was simply 'the nearest approach of mortal to supreme wisdom', which had enhanced America's reputation and made it the most imposing of civilized nations. When he turned to the issue of how the British and Europeans viewed the Constitution, he answered: 'Why, as the last hope of liberty among men. Wherever you go, you find the United States held up as an example by the advocates of freedom. The mariner no more looks to his compass or takes his departure by the sun, than does the lover of liberty think of taking his departure without reference to the constitution of the United States.'[40] Webster might have benefited from more foreign travel.

* * *

The progenitors of America's boosterish politics reflected a cultural propensity for self-promotion, which European visitors so often commented on in their travels across the United States. During his trip to North America in 1827–8, Captain Basil Hall of the Royal Navy noted the American insecurities, the longing for praise and recognition, 'all the while praising everything so highly themselves'.[41] On his tour of the United States in 1831–2, Tocqueville observed that all nations were vainglorious, but the Americans had an insatiable appetite for applause. 'They pester you at every moment to get you to praise them; and if you resist their entreaties, they praise themselves.'[42] The incessant self-promotion had a corollary that European travellers detected in America—a want of independent thought.[43] The ritual praise of the Constitution was a reflection of American conformity, which Mill, as we shall see, associated with a commercial society lacking a leisured or learned class.[44]

The cheerleaders of the US Constitution tended to perplex British political commentators, who had grown up with an unwritten, evolutionary Constitution. As citizens of an ancient state, Britons did not fully appreciate the need of the young republic for reassurance and praise. And as beneficiaries of Magna Carta, the Revolution of 1688, the Bill of Rights, and a balanced constitution, they did not like to be lectured on the origins of liberty by former colonials. Given their political history, they tended to treat constitutions not as sacred creations, but as part of the legislative process that needed amendment as circumstances warranted. A destinarian document that made claims to regulate the future in perpetuity did not conform to their experience of government.

In their zeal to appear exceptional, Americans could be accused of ignorance or selective memory, which bemused those Britons who turned their minds to political comparisons. After all, Americans had identified the British Constitution—and the House of Hanover—with civil and religious liberty for much of the eighteenth century, a point conceded by George Bancroft in his *History of the United States*.[45] Did not the colonial experience of Americans ease the translation of King, Lords, and Commons into President, Senate, and the House of Representatives? Did not that telling instrument of presidential power—the veto—resemble the royal veto, which had fallen into disuse in Britain after the reign of Queen Anne.[46] Was not the title Commander in Chief, first used by Charles I, borrowed from Britain? Did not the Congress adopt the procedures and political etiquette of Parliament? Did not American ceremonial, from inaugurations to levées, from presidential portraiture to civic pageants, imitate British monarchical traditions?[47]

Americans emphasized the originality of their Constitution, which a leading nineteenth-century historian said provided 'a complete system of government, wholly independent of tradition'.[48] But most British commentators, as we shall see, saw the document very differently, as an outgrowth of English political history. The War of Independence, after all, had been fought in defence of rights claimed by the colonists that had long been identified as part of British liberties, a point made by radicals and reformers on both sides of the Atlantic at the time of the Revolution. Did not the American Bill of Rights draw inspiration from the rights granted by Parliament following the Revolution of 1688? Americans, historians included, often fail to recall that the English Bill of Rights (1689) guaranteed the right of petition and, for Protestants at least, the right to bear arms.[49] Compare the wording of the Eighth Amendment, 'excessive bail shall not be required, nor excessive fines imposed, nor cruel and unusual punishments inflicted', with Parliament's declaration in 1689: 'excessive bail ought not to be required, nor excessive fines imposed; nor cruel and unusual punishments inflicted'.[50]

What were British commentators to make of the incessant praise of the US Constitution from scholars like Story and statesmen like Webster, which tended to relegate the British Constitution to the status of a relic? What were they to make of the metaphysical hair splitting of John C. Calhoun's *Discourse on the Constitution and Government of the United States* (1851), which defended the slaveholding interests of the South some eighty years after the Mansfield decision had made slavery unlawful in Britain, and eighteen years after its abolition throughout the British Empire? What were they to make of Orestes Brownson, the New England transcendentalist and Catholic convert, who, in *The American Republic* (1865), called the British Constitution 'feudal', while the American Constitution was 'providential, given by God himself, operating through historical events'?[51]

British radicals had been among the most fervent supporters of the American Revolution and looked upon the Constitution of the young republic with admiration, not untouched by their hopes for reform at home. They were quick to exploit the popular view that the United States was uniquely founded on the principle that the people were themselves the source of all power. The transatlantic firebrand Thomas Paine may be seen as the epitome of this tradition, and he provided powerful ammunition for those Americans who, disenchanted with the old world, found exception in the new.[52] To him America was an arcadia, a land of freedom threatened by corrupt European dynastic rivalries. In the *Rights of Man*, he argued that 'the case and circumstances of America present themselves as in the beginning of a world', for only in the United States was the Constitution 'the property of a nation, and not of those who exercise the government'.[53]

The American Revolution was an opportunity not to be missed by those who wished to reform the political system in Britain; and Paine was among those who used it as a stick to beat the mother country. The ratification of the American Constitution occurred not long before the publication of the *Rights of Man*, in which Paine dabbled in transatlantic comparative government. In his view, a constitution did not exist in England: 'A constitution is not the act of a government, but of a people constituting a government; and government without a constitution, is power without a right.' The American Constitution, 'established on the authority of the people', served as a model for mankind, which if followed would liberate Britain from the shackles of monarchical tyranny.[54]

Most Britons saw George III not as a tyrant but as a limited monarch, and given their nation's history were less inclined than Americans to make a distinction between constitutions and governments. This helps to explain why they did not see the US Constitution in a quasi-religious light. Paine's notion that 'a constitution is not an act of government' but independent of government would have seemed far-fetched to those who did not share his visceral hatred of the British monarchy. It was government, after all, that created the English Constitution over the centuries through legislation and legal precedent, a point acknowledged by the Founding Fathers and American scholars like Kent and Story, who, in contrast to Paine, did not question the existence of a British Constitution.

The study of comparative government came into sharper focus as a result of the American Revolution, and it fuelled much of the foreign interest in the United States in the nineteenth century. British commentators, whatever their political stripe, examined the American government to illuminate domestic politics; and they often invoked the United States as either a warning or a model. The Tory Dr Johnson, who hated slavery and had a hearty dislike for American independence, took a line that was gauged to embarrass the radical cause: 'How is it,' he said, 'that we always hear the loudest *yelps* for liberty amongst the drivers of negroes?'[55] Those who supported the rebellious colonists during the Revolution were typically campaigners for political reform, who set aside their dislike of slavery. The American secession, with its constitutional protection of individual liberties and free institutions, reminded them of 1688.[56] From radicals in the 1790s to Chartists in the 1840s, America had propaganda value in their campaigns for a host of issues, from universal manhood suffrage to the separation of church and state.[57]

At the other pole, British Tories treated America as a vulgar threat to aristocratic rule and combed the United States Constitution for conservative elements. Links with American loyalists, many of whom had returned to England, were often strong and provided bonds of sympathy for conservatives that countered the claims of their radical opponents. There were centrists in Britain who had a more objective view of transatlantic politics, typically professional men who were in favour of reforming an establishment they wished to enter. But whether British commentators were on the left, right, or in the centre in their interpretation of the young republic across the Atlantic, their opinions were often couched in stereotypes. Americans preferred the stereotype of their country as a marvel, prophetic of the future, but they often assumed that foreigners could never understand their form of government, and told them so.[58] On both sides of the Atlantic there was a good deal of imprecision because republicanism was increasingly being defined by radicals like Paine as democratic, though the original American Constitution was not itself democratic.[59]

In the early nineteenth century, European reactions to the American Republic continued to be deeply influenced by the French Revolution, which had divided Britons into rival camps. One of the great ironies of transatlantic affairs was that the French Revolution, heralded as another republican dawn, tended to discredit America's political experiment, even among some of those who had been sympathetic to it. In an unlikely coincidence the American Constitution went into operation at the end of April 1789, only weeks before the French Revolution began. A constitutional monarchy followed, which soon gave way to a republic, war, and the Terror. Thus something far more threatening superseded America's revolutionary experiment in the theatre of western government. The flood of refugees into London escaping revolutionary violence profoundly influenced British opinion.[60] In reactionary mood, conservatives pointed to French extremism whenever an English radical, or an American patriot, hailed a republic. In the context of the Terror and the toppled dynasties, European tumult, and the Napoleonic dictatorship that followed, republican government, including the fledgling American model, lost its charm across much of Europe.

In the decades that followed the outbreak of the French Revolution, the conservative values of Edmund Burke, who had supported the grievances of the American colonists, prevailed in Britain. Burke had defended the colonists because they were Englishmen subject to English liberties, but he lost interest in the United States once the French Revolution broke out. Tellingly, he did not make constitutional comparisons between America and France in *Reflections on the Revolution in France* (1790). But he observed in a parliamentary debate in 1791 that Americans were suited for republican government, not only because 'they had a certain quantity of phlegm, of old English good nature that suited them better for it', but because their education as colonists had been under a government already strongly republican. While he would have preferred the general model of the 1688–9 settlement to a written constitution, the Americans had 'formed their government, as nearly as they could, according to the model of the British Constitution'.[61]

As the example of Burke suggests, the French Revolution eclipsed the American Revolution in the European mind. French politics so scarred generations of Britons that it was still being used as a warning against republican excess in the 1880s.[62] In the decades of reaction after 1789, British radicals still looked to America for sustenance, but support for its republican government became more muted among them. This was politic in a nation in which the French Revolution had turned 'republicanism' into the most hated word in the lexicon of British patriots. The association of a republic with political chaos and a violent usurpation of property shadowed the promise of American democracy.[63] Against the background of war and revolution, of inertia and reaction, the radical project fell away in Britain. Apart from the conservative backlash, the issue of Anglo-American trade remained fraught as well in the 1790s, which the Napoleonic Wars exacerbated in the early years of the new century.

As freshly minted Americans lauded their Constitution in the early decades of the republic, British interest in the American government waned. The French Revolution had taken the gloss off republicanism, while the Napoleonic Wars diminished the ease of commerce and communication between the two nations. Arguably America's reputation in Europe was at its lowest ebb during the presidencies of Jefferson and Madison, a reputation not helped by the name of Jefferson's party, whose official title, the Democratic-Republican Party, suggested sympathy with the French Republic. The War of 1812 put a further brake on Anglo-American relations, and when the flaccid and disputatious Latin American republics appeared in the 1820s, they did little to further the republican cause in Europe.

As events both inside and outside America diminished the reputation of republican ideals, official relations between Britain and the United States deteriorated in an era of increased diplomatic tension.[64] British officials often took a peremptory attitude towards Americans in the early nineteenth century for reasons of diplomacy as well as New World republicanism.[65] Meanwhile, all but the most ardent radicals became less vocal in their support of their liberal cousins across the Atlantic. Positive references to America in Parliament turned on the relatively low cost of its government, an issue that had animated Paine, who had savaged the British monarchy for its expense in the *Rights of Man*. In 1816, at the height of the Civil List debate in Parliament, the Whig reformer Lord Holland asked for a comparison with the cost of American government. 'God forbid that we, who were not republicans, should compare ourselves with a republican government', he observed. But following Paine's lead, he found America useful in the campaign for economical reform.[66]

The issue of slavery further complicated transatlantic relations. It was well known in Britain that many of the presidents in the early decades of the republic were slave owners, including Washington, Jefferson, Madison, and Monroe; it was a point raised, as we shall see, by John Stuart Mill. In reviewing a book on American statistics in the *Edinburgh Review* in 1820, the English clergyman and wit Sydney Smith asked: 'under which of the old tyrannical governments of Europe is every sixth man a Slave, whom his fellow-creatures may buy and sell and torture'?[67] Slavery was a practice little noted by the proponents of American exceptionalism in the early years of the republic, but much despised by British visitors.[68] Indeed, slavery was the measure of American democracy for many of them, who saw such disregard for human suffering at odds with the equality of man proclaimed in the Declaration of Independence. In the 1830s, the American Minister in London, Andrew Stevenson of Virginia, was still defending slavery, which did not endear him to his British hosts.[69] Victorian critics questioned whether America was, after all, a democracy, when millions of slaves were disfranchised and treated with such contempt.[70]

While Britons approved or disapproved of former colonials trumpeting their republican ideals, Americans were forging a new world identity under the umbrella of their English origins. The superiority of republican government to hereditary monarchy became a staple of American propaganda. George III continued to be wheeled out to frighten the children on the Fourth of July; but cultural bonds remained very powerful and even the King underwent a reassessment in the republic. At his death in 1820 he was widely hailed in the American press as a Christian gentleman and decent family man, who was steadfast in the face of French tyranny. 'Anglo-Saxonism'—the links of language, law, and ancestry—trumped Jacobin principles. While Americans rhetorically denounced the perfidy of monarchy or dismissed the British Constitution as 'feudal', it did not diminish the fascination with which they followed royal events in the mother country.[71] As one American worthy noted, 'no community worships hereditary rank and station like a democracy'.[72]

Meanwhile, many British subjects continued to see the United States as the wayward offspring of the mother country. Where Americans saw differences, they saw resemblances, not least in their forms of government. Republicanism itself was a shapeless idea, which, as the Founding Fathers were aware, had been applied to Britain's limited monarchy.[73] By the mid-nineteenth century, it was not uncommon in Britain and America to see the President of the United States as an elective monarch, modelled on George III but with a fixed term.[74] This was the constitutional counterpart of seeing Americans as little more than provincial Englishmen, which was a view widely held in Britain well into the nineteenth century. 'The people of the United States are *provincial*', wrote Mill, '... In all matters social or literary, they are a province of the British empire. This peculiarity of position, to which even their descent contributes, is indissolubly fixed by the identity of language.'[75] Having met some Americans in Italy, he wrote to his wife Harriet: 'I never saw such complete John Bulls as some of them.... Their twang was *exactly* that of provincial English.'[76]

Americans remained deeply indebted to the English language and culture, but as they took on their own national character, they paraded their republican principles and resented being seen as John Bulls. One can only imagine the American response to reading that they were transplanted rustics—only touchy and unoriginal. What were they to make of the best-selling travel book *Domestic Manners of the Americans* (1832), in which Mrs Trollope took a patrician attitude to Americans, whom she dismissed as misguided Englishmen who praised their democracy while tormenting their slaves? 'I do not like their principles, I do not like their manners, I do not like their opinions.'[77] And what were they to make of her son, the novelist Anthony Trollope, who thirty years later called the American 'thin skinned' and given to self-idolatry? 'Any touch comes at once upon the net-work of his nerves and puts in operation all his organs of feeling with the violence of a blow.'[78]

Given their assumption that Americans were unsophisticated Englishmen abroad, who had inherited their language, laws, and liberty from the mother country, many British writers were ill-disposed to see the United States as a unique political experiment. Forty years after the Declaration of Independence, the poet Samuel Taylor Coleridge did not recognize an America independent of Britain because of the bonds of language and culture.[79] Rather, he likened the destiny of America to 'Great Britain in a state of glorious magnification!'[80] During his tour of the United States in 1842, Charles Dickens found the mass of Americans hospitable, assertive, and humourless, but noted the political similarities between the two nations.[81] In 1850, the essayist and historian Thomas Carlyle, not an admirer of American democracy, remarked that the US 'Constitution, such as it may be, was made here, not there; went over with them from the Old-Puritan, English workshop, ready-made'.[82]

The two nations were bound—some have said separated—by a common language and a common history, which fuelled affection, curiosity, misunderstanding, and sometimes derision. Wars, diplomatic tensions, and economic rivalries often strained relations in the nineteenth century. But for nearly two hundred years the colonists had been subjects of the Crown, and this gave the British a proprietary interest in their American cousins. As transatlantic travel eased in the 1820s and 1830s, the availability of knowledge about America expanded in Europe. Increasingly, British commentators began to write with more information about the US government, which had been difficult to come by during the Napoleonic Wars when transatlantic relations and lines of communication were more fraught. They did so with that mixture of tolerance and disapproval characteristic of members of an extended family.

In the decades from the 1820s on, scores of articles appeared on America in the leading British periodicals, from the Tory *Quarterly* to the Whig *Edinburgh Review* to the radical *Westminster Review*.[83] They advanced their competing visions of America but did not provide anything like a sustained analysis of the US Constitution. News about America, though on the increase, was often misinformed. Before Mill's reviews of Tocqueville's *Democracy in America*, discussions of American government by British writers were pretty elementary. The utilitarian Jeremy Bentham (1748–1832), whose influence was to be seen in the *Westminster Review*, wrote frequently about America, but his analysis was unsystematic and often superficial, lapsing into an idealistic stereotype without much technical knowledge.[84] More than once he called the Secretary of State the Home Secretary, which typified the difficulty that British commentators had in getting outside their own political culture.[85]

Bentham initially opposed the American Revolution and described the Declaration of Independence as 'a hodge podge of confusion and absurdity in which the theory to be proved is all along taken for granted'.[86] For him, government was the only source of rights, and he dismissed the natural rights embedded in American state constitutions as fanciful. But while American liberalism and English utilitarianism were strange bedfellows, Bentham saw utility in praising American democracy in the interest of British radicalism; for whatever its faults, the United States provided prosperity for its citizens and repudiated the dross and corruption of aristocracy and monarchy.[87] Thus he hailed the US Constitution as an Anglo-American success story and described himself as a 'Philo-Yankee'.[88] If the English government was the 'least bad', that of the United States was 'the first of all governments to which the epithet of good, in the positive sense of the word, could, with propriety be attached'.[89]

As the American states extended the suffrage to all white males in the early nineteenth century, its system of government became ever more newsworthy, whatever one's politics. The levelling spirit of Jacksonian democracy, widely noted in Europe, was on the rise, with uncertain consequences for both the United States and the mother country. In the late 1820s and early 1830s, an era of reform on both sides of the Atlantic, various British writers, including Radicals, Tories and Whigs, disputed the nature of American democracy, often with more heat than light as they fitted the facts to suit their principles. Radicals tended to ignore the undemocratic features of the US Constitution in favour of talking about democracy as a social condition. In their view, the contrast between democratic values and oligarchic rule would bring the inequalities of Britain into disrepute. To many Conservatives, such contrasts were meaningless, for the circumstances of the United States were unique. In their assessment, American prosperity had less to do with political equality than with natural resources, a low population, and the absence of public debt.[90] The United States government came into sharper focus during the agitation surrounding the Reform Bill of 1832, which enlivened the political debate in Britain. Whigs and Radicals stepped up their praise of America in the campaign for reform, while the conservatives, fearful of propaganda from across the Atlantic, made the case against democracy with equal vigour. As the case for democratic reform picked up steam, conservatives emphasized the continuities in American politics and history and dismissed the notion that the Founding Fathers had devised any novel principles. They assumed that the American Constitution owed more to Anglo-Saxon pragmatism than to European ideas of popular sovereignty. In 1833, the Tory historian Archibald Alison, no friend to radical experiments, noted in *Blackwood's* that the 'impatient spirit and interminable expectations of the people' made it of 'incalculable importance' that America should be seen in its 'true colours'.[91] What constituted these 'true colours' would preoccupy British writers for decades.

The ancestral and historic links between the two great English-speaking peoples ensured that America, the world's ascendant democracy, was worthy of reflection—and partisan analysis. In the nineteenth century, Europeans travelled to America rather as western observers travelled to Russia in the 1920s and 1930s, to witness a great political experiment.[92] Between 1835 and 1860, over 200 British visitors retailed their new world experiences in print.[93] American commentators were highly sensitive to their views, not least those with a political agenda, because they cared so much for British good opinion. Meanwhile, cultural connections with the United States encouraged British travellers to press American trends into service for partisan purposes in an age of incipient democracy at home. But the more they learnt about government and politics in the United States, the more complex democracy appeared and the stereotypes began to give way to more sophisticated analyses that challenged the assumptions of the political parties back in Britain.

One of the more notable English authors who visited America in the mid-1830s was Harriet Martineau, the daughter of a Unitarian textile manufacturer from Norwich, who is best remembered for her popular writings on political economy and her translation of Auguste Comte.[94] She travelled widely in the United States, and the result was *Society in America*, published in three volumes in 1837. The book was not a comparison of British and American politics, but it did provide a critique of the United States in keeping with the views of the *Westminster Review*, which she leavened with descriptions of the country and its people. While she was full of enthusiasm for the liberal experiment, she did little to reinforce the radical stereotype of America as a Utopia. Americans, in her opinion, had not yet created a 'national character' and their 'veneration for England', though natural, was excessive. Her main criticism was that 'the civilisation and the morals of the Americans fall below their own principles'.[95]

Society in America was yet another example of seeing America through British eyes, in Martineau's case through a radical lens, which equated aristocracy with fear-mongering and democracy with expectation. As her leading biographer noted, the book 'appeared sound in structure and hopeful in policy, but in political spirit it was sadly defective'.[96] It was an early contribution to the British debate on democratic principles, but one that did not much rise above a party pamphlet. As Martineau saw it, America contradicted those conservative sceptics who believed mankind did not have a capacity for self-government. While she thought it too early to tell whether the experiment would measure up to the rhetoric of American patriots, the Constitution worked well enough to encourage optimism about democracy, despite its tearful compromise over slavery.

While admired in England, *Society in America* did not amuse readers in the United States, who challenged her facts while dismissing her generalizations. One critic described her as an 'ugly, deaf, sour old crabapple'.[97] Martineau had, after all, accused Americans of a 'deficiency of moral independence' and said they reminded her of the Irish.[98] The book was something of a hybrid, part social treatise, part moral tract, with chapters on the economy, rural labour, and religion. It was most notable for its adherence to the Abolitionist campaign and women's rights, causes in their infancy in the 1830s. Her chapters on government were strangely inconsequential, given that she had talked to leading American politicians, including James Madison, who convinced her that the United States had been 'useful in proving things before held impossible'. Another statesman convinced her that the

INTRODUCTION: TRANSATLANTIC ATTITUDES 21

Senate was 'only a temporary affair; an accident', which was soon to undergo a radical overhaul. Her view of the executive was also a little off centre, for during the height of the Jackson administration, she took the view that presidential influence had subsided into something 'very weak and transitory'.[99] Meanwhile, his American critics were calling him 'King Andrew the First'.[100]

A comparison of Martineau's *Society in America* with the first volume of Tocqueville's *Democracy in America* (1835) springs to mind—but not to the former's advantage. The two travellers visited many of the same places in the United States and probably met some of the same people. Martineau was, in fact, far ahead of the Frenchman on the issue of women's rights and more engaged in the campaign to abolish slavery. But as she said of herself, she could popularize but had limited powers of the imagination and 'nothing approaching genius'.[101] One cannot look to her for a theory of US society, which perhaps explains her neglect of the more speculative Tocqueville, who is not mentioned in *Society in America*. This was, however, a singular omission since the political class in Britain was talking about his views when her book appeared.

Tocqueville's expansive analysis of the United States was to have profound repercussions for transatlantic attitudes. The leading Victorian thinkers on American government all read *Democracy in America*, which, to varying degrees, shaped their reaction to the United States. By the 1840s, democracy, not anti-monarchy, largely defined the idea of republicanism in Britain.[102] It was a view that Tocqueville reinforced by using the appellation democracy or 'democratic republic' to describe America. Indeed, one of the chief effects of his book was to cement the growing linkage of republicanism and democracy in the minds of British thinkers, whether they assessed democracy as a social condition or a set of political arrangements. While many nineteenth-century Americans described their country as a republic—and some still do—Victorian writers preferred to use the word democracy, which was less confusing to the British public, many of whom thought they lived in a republic, albeit a monarchical one.[103]

Those eminent Victorians who wrote most extensively, and acutely, on American democracy—Mill in the 1830s–1860s, Walter Bagehot in the 1860s, and Sir Henry Maine and James Bryce in the 1880s—glimpsed the future of Britain across the Atlantic. They wished to know whether the experiment in America was a success and whether it prefigured the political fate of Britain's aristocratic government, which was increasingly under threat from political reform at home. If democracy were the future how were its vices to be attenuated and its virtues bestowed? The nineteenth century was a battleground of ideas. After the revolutions in America and France, the task of political thought was one of reconstruction. In their search for answers to the critical issue of democracy the Victorians provided some of the most penetrating appraisals of the evolution of American government and society. Their writings may also be seen as part of the ongoing Anglo-American debate over the origins and soul of democracy.

2

John Stuart Mill
The Tyranny of Conformity

> In the American democracy, the aristocracy of skin, and the aristocracy of sex, retain their privileges.
>
> (John Stuart Mill, 1835)
>
> The natural tendency of representative government, as of modern civilization, is towards collective mediocrity.
>
> (John Stuart Mill, 1861)

A principal cause of the revival of British interest in the United States was the publication of Alexis de Tocqueville's *Democracy in America*, which received glittering reviews in a host of British periodicals. The timing of the book was propitious, for it coincided with an era of political agitation in Britain.[1] The first volume appeared in 1835, not long after the Reform Act of 1832 widened the franchise to the middle classes and opened up the prospect of further reform. The second volume appeared in 1840, during a peak in the Chartist campaign for the extension of democratic rights. After reading Tocqueville, few British commentators doubted that the American experiment was a portent of the future. One influential review announced: 'the era of democracy has begun'.[2] Another, paraphrasing Tocqueville, observed that a democratic revolution was under way that would soon spread to Europe.[3]

It may seem ironic that Tocqueville, a French aristocrat, was open to American democracy. But he was part of what the poet Alfred de Musset called a lost generation, for he came of age after the failure of the France's revolutionary hopes and the demise of its Napoleonic ambitions. The very failings of his class made his intellectual journey to the United States irresistible. He crossed the Atlantic to illuminate a grand idea, the gradual development in western civilization of the principle of equality, which he took to be inevitable. His coolness in dissecting the American republic was all the more impressive given that members of his family had been guillotined during the French Revolution. When asked how he maintained his composure in his analysis of America, given the disturbed intellectual climate in Europe, he replied: 'had you, like me, been bred up in the midst of revolutions and counter-revolutions, despotisms, restorations, and all the miseries of insecurity, political and personal, you might have learned to view the worst that passes in America with calmness'.[4]

Like his master Montesquieu, Tocqueville admired the English and the English Constitution and acknowledged the importance of comparative analysis. Like many British commentators on the United States he saw his primary audience as his fellow countrymen, not Americans, a point often noticed by US reviewers.[5] The meaning of American democracy for Europe, particularly France, was never far from his mind. By the time of his book's publication, so many visitors had been to America that it was no longer seen as a backwater on the edge of civilization but the nation of the future. What set him apart from the likes of Basil Hall, Harriet Martineau, and Mrs Trollope was a determination to ask serious sociological questions. What were the effects of social organization on politics and what were their implications for the advance of liberty? What Tocqueville achieved was to shift political inquiry from narrow constitutional issues to the wider society.

British reviewers of *Democracy in America* were struck by the book's detachment, and they noted that Tocqueville's approach was in stark contrast with other commentators on the United States, whose purpose was so often to advance some dogma or to expand on some favoured philosophical principle. The conservative *Quarterly Review* censured American writers in particular, who were even more unreliable than foreigners: 'For they are all party men; and so vehemently do they feel interested in the honour of their country, that their judgment is almost inevitably distorted by their anxiety, at all hazards, to promulgate certain opinions.'[6] The result of these distortions had been to introduce mistaken ideas about the condition of America in Europe. What Tocqueville provided was a new foundation on which to explore democracy in the United States and beyond, freed from the long cherished fallacies and the 'red hot excitations' of Americans themselves, whose purpose in writing was not detached analysis but 'to fuse their nation into one mass'.[7] While Tocqueville was composing *Democracy in America*, John Stuart Mill was busy editing the *London Review*, a new journal intended to provide a voice for the cause of philosophical radicalism. At the time Mill was forging his reputation as the most thoughtful proponent of liberalism in England. The first volume of *Democracy in America*, which he reviewed in the summer of 1835, gave him an opportunity to explore an issue of paramount importance to the radical cause. He found the work a brilliant contrast to the customary British writings on America, which were party pamphlets disguised as travel books.[8] To Mill, England and the United States were among the great nations of the world, but each had some grievous defects from which the other was exempt. Tocqueville provided just the hoped-for impartial, systematic study of America that would enlarge the discussion of democracy and counter partisan views.

If Tocqueville wrote dispassionately about the United States not all his readers followed his lead. In England, as elsewhere, observers seized on facts that suited their values, while political parties converted Tocqueville's analysis to party purposes.[9] In this sense, British commentators, setting objectivity aside, often fell into the same trap into which Americans had fallen. This was a point made by Mill in his essay on volume two of *Democracy in America*, which appeared in the *Edinburgh Review* in 1840: 'The progress of political dissatisfaction, and comparisons made between the fruits of a popular constitution on one side of the Atlantic, and of a mixed government with a preponderating aristocratic element on the other, had made the working of American institutions a party question.'[10]

One of the things Mill admired about *Democracy in America* was that it provided a new model of comparative government free from party prejudice, which introduced 'a new era in the scientific study of politics'.[11] The structure that shaped Tocqueville's analysis was not American party politics, which he largely avoided, but the contrast between aristocracy and democracy. Mill mirrored this structure in his reviews. America had become a focus of political traditions that divided Europe into partisan camps. 'Democrats have sought to prove', observed Mill, '... that we ought to be democrats; aristocrats, that we should cleave to aristocracy, and withstand the democratic spirit.'[12]

His own liberal assessment was that while Tocqueville's conclusions leaned 'towards radicalism', Tories found phrases like 'the tyranny of the majority' to their liking and turned the Frenchman into 'one of the pillars of Conservatism'.[13]

What Mill thought important about *Democracy in America* was not simply its subtlety and method but the protean nature of its arguments. Tocqueville treated democracy as something real and not an abstraction. He said that he wished to examine with precision all the mechanisms of American society that everyone discusses yet no one understands. Mill, who thought Tocqueville's mind resembled Montesquieu's but with 'superadded good sense', took him at his word.[14] 'It is not risking too much to affirm of these volumes, that they contain the first analytical inquiry into the influence of democracy.' As Mill saw it, American democracy was so pregnant with meaning and endless in its ramifications 'that he who sees furthest into them will longest hesitate before finally pronouncing whether the good or evil of its influence, on the whole, preponderates'.[15]

Tocqueville concluded that democracy had been advancing since the dawn of time and was inevitable and desirable, but only under certain conditions, which were capable of being realized or frustrated. His belief that democracy was synonymous with 'equality of conditions' and the absence of an aristocracy was a challenging idea to the British, where a landed aristocracy was still powerful and social hierarchy remained entrenched. Mill was much taken with the view that across Europe all nations were moving towards the extension of political rights and the removal of distinctions based on hereditary wealth. But he felt Tocqueville made a serious error in confusing 'the effects of Democracy with the effects of Civilization. He has bound up in one abstract idea the whole of the tendencies of modern commercial society, and given them one name—Democracy; thereby letting it be supposed that he ascribes to equality of conditions, several of the effects naturally arising from the mere progress of national prosperity.'[16]

Like Tocqueville, Mill admired much about American society: its enterprise, its active citizenry, its free associations, its local self-government, and its judicial system. He associated democracy with prosperity and 'government of a numerous middle class', but he did not assume, coming from a relatively open, albeit aristocratic society, that it was incompatible with social hierarchy, or for that matter with monarchy. Democratic America was altogether middle class in Mill's view, whereas in Britain the ascendant middle class, though not a numerical majority, was increasingly shaping government. Tocqueville saw equality of conditions as the prominent feature of American democracy, but Mill did not see much sign of it in Britain, where there was little enthusiasm for egalitarianism.[17] By emphasizing the flexibility and middle-class nature of democracy he made it more amenable to an English audience that was chary of further suffrage reform after the 1832 Reform Act.

Like Tocqueville, Mill moved easily between discussions of democratic institutions and wider social issues, and he had serious criticisms of the particular form of democracy taking shape in America. But he saw advantages, which stemmed from his education at the hands of the Utilitarians. The course of legislation tended to benefit the greatest number of people. He felt that the United States could support the transitory effects of bad laws and mediocre public servants even when legislation was defective. Much in America, as he recognized, turned not on legal and democratic causes but on the nation's special circumstances: its natural resources, its open spaces, and the lack of extreme wealth or poverty, points that conservatives often made.[18] Mill also noted the perpetual exercise of the faculties among the American public, which Tocqueville had witnessed: 'I have no doubt that the democratic institutions of the United States, joined to the physical constitution of the country, are the cause... of the prodigious commercial activity of the inhabitants. It is not engendered by the laws, but it proceeds from habits acquired through participation in making the laws.'[19]

In Mill's political philosophy, habit was an important consideration, not least when linked with local self-government and voluntary activity, what Tocqueville called the 'habit of association'. Mill might have been thinking of America when, in an essay on Bentham before the publication of *Democracy in America*, he suggested that the acquiescence of voters in their elective governments was the effect of mere habit, a consequence of their desire for institutional continuity, even when it did not serve their interests.[20] But, like Tocqueville, he applauded the habit of active citizenship, which was necessary to popular government. The long tradition of serving in popular local institutions was, after all, a reason for the organic development of democracy in Britain:

only by the habit of superintending their local interests can the diffusion of intelligence and mental activity, as applied to their joint concerns, take place among the mass of a people, which can qualify them to superintend with steadiness or consistency the proceedings of their government, or to exercise any power in national affairs except by fits, and as tools in the hands of others.[21]

Given his liberal emphasis on participatory citizenship, Mill was particularly impressed by Tocqueville's discussion of an aspect of political life in America little understood in Europe—municipal government. Mill described it as 'the fountain-head of American democracy'.[22] For Tocqueville, the New England municipal system, with its plethora of functionaries, was a revelation, the foundation of a democratic society. It was to liberty, he said, 'what primary education was to science'.[23] It divided the local authority broadly among the residents and did not scruple to multiply their obligations, reminding them that they belonged to a community, and by extension to government more generally. To Mill, Tocqueville's analysis of this issue was of paramount importance. Neither of them pretended that the New England model of municipal government could be copied in Europe, but as democracy spread around the world the need for more enlightened local self-government was urgent, both as a school and as a 'safety-valve'.[24]

Tocqueville found faults in American institutions, but he considered the Federal Constitution, with its checks and balances, a work of sagacity drawn up by men of foresight. Mill agreed, though not unquestioningly. He noted that the institutional mainspring of America was the principle of sharing the powers of municipal, state, and Federal government among a great variety of elected officials and keeping these independent of one another. But such a system of divided sovereignty, capped by the tripartite division of power in the Federal government between the President, the Senate, and the House of Representatives, each independent of one another, suffered from being so often in opposition. 'In what manner is harmony maintained among these jarring elements', he asked. 'How is so minute a division of the government power rendered compatible with the existence of government'?[25]

Mill recognized that a common superior—the people—periodically elected all the independent officials in their respective spheres. As a consequence, no one wished to collide with any co-ordinate authority unless he believed that his constituents would approve his conduct. Still, this check did not suffice in all cases, for the authorities were accountable to different constituencies. In disputes between municipal officers and the state government, or between a state and the Federal government, the constituents of competing parties might support their representatives in a quarrel. 'Moreover, the check often operates too slowly, and is not of a sufficiently energetic character for the graver delinquencies.'[26]

The supreme arbiter between members of the divided sovereignty—the American judiciary—was to provide a remedy. Not only were executive officers answerable to the courts for acts done in their public capacity, but the legislatures themselves were as well. (In the *Marbury v. Madison* case of 1803, the Supreme Court established that judges had the power of judicial review, which was an issue not explicitly addressed in the Constitution.) The Court could not punish a legislature for having overstepped its authority, but it could set aside its acts, and it was empowered to strike down any law, state or federal, deemed to be unconstitutional. Mill asked, rather rhetorically, whether the Supreme Court's remarkable authority rendered the Constitution of the United States 'unalterable'? Furthermore, did judges, who wielded such great power, impede government, rather in the manner of the House of Lords?[27]

Mill answered both questions in the negative. The Constitution could be amended in a manner prescribed by the Constitution. The courts were powerless to repeal constitutional amendments, but in the mean time their control prevented the letter and spirit of the Constitution from being infringed upon. Nor did Mill believe that the judges had irresponsible power conferred upon them as legislators of the last resort. He agreed with Tocqueville that the framers of the Constitution had understood that in a working democracy powers might safely be entrusted to the courts:

A judge is one of the most deadly instruments in the hands of a tyranny of which others are at the head; but, while he can only exercise political influence through the indirect medium of judicial decisions, he acts within too confined a sphere for it to be possible for him to establish a despotism in his own favour. The Americans saw that courts of justice, without a monarchy or an aristocracy to back them, could never oppose any permanent obstacle to the will of the people.[28]

To Mill, every government had to have a supreme arbiter, to keep the peace between the various authorities. In the American system, the Founding Fathers recognized the danger in making the political or electoral branches arbiters of the Constitution and thus created a moderating power in the courts. They granted considerable power to the courts, but diminished it by debarring them from the use of it except by judicial means. This was sensible to Mill, who believed the framers had forged a legal system amenable to democracy and favourable to liberty. He did not, however, think judges should be irremovable and thought their popular election, introduced by some of the State Constitutions, was one of a democracy's most perilous errors.[29] Still, he quoted Tocqueville on the judicial system at length and with approval: 'the power vested in the American courts of justice of pronouncing a statute to be unconstitutional, forms one of the most powerful barriers, which has ever been devised against the tyranny of political assemblies'.[30]

For all the virtues of American democracy, Mill pinpointed what he saw as its many failings, which included the election of judges and the appointment of officials on grounds of patronage rather than qualifications. Like most European commentators, he was unimpressed by US politicians, who were often ignorant, philistine, and ill prepared for public service. (Unlike Congressmen, British MPs were unpaid before 1911 and were thus drawn from the leisured class.) Mill agreed with Tocqueville that 'the race of American statesman has decidedly dwarfed within the last half-century'.[31] Like other critics, he thought the electoral system promoted mediocrity in political candidates, not least for the presidency, and that Americans were largely indifferent to merit in elections, while the turnover of legislators was rapid. Moreover, almost any other career held out better financial rewards to a man of ability. In America 'statesmanship is not a profession . . . there are no traditions, no science or art of public affairs'.[32]

Mill conceded that visionary politicians were the exception in most nations. Even in Britain, where power resided in the Prime Minister and his cabinet, the frequent changes of government meant that far-sighted views of policy were rarely acted upon. In an international crisis like the American Revolution, the choice of the people fell to the first men in the country. But given the current peaceful state of affairs and their limited responsibilities in the world, Americans might be said to be sensible 'not to pay the price of great talents when common ones will serve their purpose'. According to Mill, writing over two decades before the outbreak of the Civil War, America needed very little government. Unlike European countries 'she has no wars, no neighbours, no complicated international relations; no old society with its thousand abuses to reform; no half-fed and untaught millions crying for food and guidance. Society in America requires little but to be let alone.'[33]

Being 'let alone' was not a given, however. To Tocqueville, American democracy had the potential to produce a new form of despotism that interfered in the cycle of private interests. A revolution against aristocratic power brought with it a strong spirit of independence, but as the principle of equality emerged, it gradually brought with it a propensity to strengthen and centralize government. It was ironic, as Tocqueville observed, that men 'sought to be free in order to make themselves equal; but in proportion as equality was more established by the aid of freedom, freedom itself was thereby rendered more difficult of attainment'. At issue was whether America would create a 'tyranny of the majority' that 'would degrade men without tormenting them'.[34]

Mill questioned Tocqueville's generalization about the despotism of the majority, in part because he didn't think America required the degree of government that would encourage it to tyrannize the public. But his chief criticism of Tocqueville's idea was that it was simply an observation without evidence to support it. America was not like Europe where class divisions, real or imaginary, represented a danger to property or contracts. What would induce the greater number in America to oppress the smaller? He seconded Tocqueville's view that the rich and poor were not at odds. Where everyone had property or the hope of enjoying a large fortune through exertion, the inviolability of property was a given. Mill assumed, rather innocently given the growing wealth of the moneyed men in the commercial cities, that the rich in America were content to be rich and did not claim any particular political influence.[35] Both he and Tocqueville tended to exaggerate the economic equality in the United States, which blinded them to the dangers of plutocracy.

As Mill saw it, it was not a separation of interests that endangered minorities in America, but the nation's 'antipathies of religion, political party, or race'.[36] The tyranny of the majority would not be a result of despotic laws but 'that of dispensing power over all laws'. He gave several examples, including the citizens of New York and Philadelphia, who sacked the houses of the Abolitionists and the schools of their black fellow-citizens with impunity.[37] It was disturbing because of the impossibility of obtaining the aid of the police or the justice of the courts, but also because of the apathy and cowardice of the onlookers who watched in silence:

> For where the majority is the sole power, and a power issuing its mandates in the form of riots, it inspires a terror which the most arbitrary monarch often fails to excite. The silent sympathy of the majority may support on the scaffold the martyr of one man's tyranny; but if we would imagine the situation of a victim of the majority itself, we must look to the annals of religious persecution for a parallel.[38]

Tocqueville argued that in the United States equality of condition had reached its ultimate limit and democracy reigned undisputed. Mill agreed that there was much to be said for this assertion, but the properties of democracy, both good and bad, were evident in the test bed of America. What most disturbed him was that so many Americans were excluded from politics, most notably slaves, who were 'ruthlessly excluded in some States by law, and the remainder by actual bodily fear'.[39] Social equality was a chimera when 'no white person will sit at the same table with them, or on the same bench in a public room'.[40] He concluded that as far as the slave states were concerned it was a perversion to call America a democracy.[41]

In a review article 'State of Society in America' (1836), Mill noted that many of the nation's most eminent founders had come from a slaveholding class of leisured gentlemen. And he asked why there were no successors to the Washingtons and Jeffersons, the Madisons and Monroes, in an age far superior to theirs in intellectual resources and facilities? He argued that the families that gave birth to these men were the beneficiaries of slave labour in the then prosperous state of Virginia. As the prosperity of Virginia declined, 'the stream has ceased to flow, because its fountain is dried up'.[42] He did not know why other slave states had not thrown up men of equal excellence. Nor did he explore the irony in his argument that, while slavery fostered a leisured class that he believed essential to extend the benefits of democracy, the very existence of slavery was incompatible with democracy.

Like slavery, the question of women's rights was becoming central to Mill's thinking in the 1830s; and in reviewing *Democracy in America* he linked the issue of race prejudice to the position of women in society. Tocqueville, who was content to see women in a domestic role, was not an enthusiast for expanding their political rights. As he put it, 'in America the independence of woman is irretrievably lost within the bonds of marriage'.[43] But to Mill, there was no excuse to exclude women from the vote since their destiny was as dependent on elections as the destiny of men. It was a signal abuse that in the world's premier democracy 'one entire half of the human race is wholly excluded from the political equality so much boasted of, and that in point of social equality their position is still more dependent than in Europe. In the American democracy, the aristocracy of skin, and the aristocracy of sex, retain their privileges.'[44]

In 1838, Lincoln had condemned America's 'mobocratic spirit', which had little regard for the laws and led to the hanging of slaves, minorities, and strangers.[45] Mill, who would come to revere Lincoln, also abhorred acts of lawless power, but he observed that 'in America tyranny will seldom use the instrument of law, because among the white population there is no permanent class to be tyrannized over'.[46] The subjects of oppression, the whites among them at least, were the casual objects of popular anger and the majority would discover in time that it could not enjoy the advantages of civilized society while taking men's lives and property at its discretion. He assumed that such crimes would diminish as minorities fought for their interests and the majority did not wish to incite them. Within the limits of civil life, the despotism of the majority, though a genuine evil, did not appear very alarming to Mill.

Mill was unusual in his day in thinking a denial of freedom was more likely to come from social oppression than political despotism.[47] He believed that the tyranny to be feared in America, at least for the white population, was 'a tyranny not over the body but over the mind'.[48] In no country, he asserted, was there less independence of thought, which was a precondition for individual freedom. In Mill's opinion, the reason the US Constitution tolerated religious freedom was because of the variety of religious denominations.'If by ill fortune there had happened to be a religion of the majority, the case would probably have been different.'[49] On other issues the conventional wisdom prevailed, leading to a tyranny of conformity, a society in which scarcely any person had the courage to dissent.

The conformity of life in the United States dismayed Mill. Though familiar with the *Federalist* papers and the writings of the Founding Fathers, he makes no mention of early American historians or the legal authorities like Kent or Story, who might have given him some clues on the pressure for consensus in a nation-building society.[50] What disturbed him was that few Americans had the courage to say anything disrespectful on issues once approved by the general public.[51] The lack of dissent led to a passive citizenry who followed the received wisdom 'with the most servile adulation and sycophancy'.[52] On this point, Mill's language was less colourful than that of Tocqueville, who argued, in a famous passage, that democratic governments threatened to stupefy a people, 'and finally each nation is reduced to being nothing more than a herd of timid and industrious animals of which the government is the shepherd'.[53]

Democracy in America gave Mill an opportunity to make comparisons with Britain, both politically and socially, and he found many resemblances. Like other Victorians he applauded the Anglo-American talent for creating effective constitutions. 'Whatever other faults have been found with the Anglo-American constitutions, no one has yet said that they will not *work*; a fate so often denounced against all constitutions except those which, like the British, "are made but grow".' Constitutions that did not work, he concluded, were made '*for* the people, while those which do work, such as the American, are made *by* the people'.[54] To Mill, democracy was immanent in colonial institutions. Unlike American exceptionalists, he believed that when the thirteen states had been colonies they 'were, as to internal government, nearly as complete democracies as they are now'.[55]

While mid-Victorian England was not notable for equality of conditions, Mill believed that nearly all the moral and social influences that Tocqueville found in middle-class America were in operation in aristocratic England. He noted other similarities: the expansion of industry, the commercialization of society, the growing insignificance of individuals, and the power of the middle class. The ascendancy of the commercial class in modern society and politics was inevitable, but not necessarily an evil. 'Now, as ever, the great problem in government is to prevent the strongest from becoming the only power; and repress the natural tendency of the instincts and passions of the ruling body to sweep away all barriers which are capable of resisting, even for a moment, their own tendencies.'[56]

Mill felt it a fanciful hope to check the rising power of the commercial interest, but as an Englishman he consoled himself that there were two classes in Britain largely absent in America that counterbalanced the potential tyranny of the business community—the leisured and learned classes.[57] Mill expressed the typical disdain Europeans had for American culture when he called New York and Boston provincial cities of the British Empire in regard to learning and letters.[58] He believed that the United States, though endowed with theologians and universities, lacked an intellectual aristocracy, which put the future of American democracy in peril. He seconded Tocqueville's opinion that mediocrity reigned in respect to knowledge in America and that there was no class that relished intellectual pleasure, nor a hereditary affluence that honoured the life of the mind.[59] This was no small matter to

Mill, who believed that the intelligence of the citizenry was 'the first element of good government'.[60]

Both Mill and Tocqueville, like so many other Europeans of their generation, saw Americans as displaced Englishmen, but lacking the Englishman's intellectual vitality and independence of thought. In their writings we may see the beginnings of the perception that the United States was inhospitable to intellectuals.[61] They were well aware that Americans themselves—at least the cultivated classes—recognized their dependence on the mother country. As Coleridge observed in his *Specimens of Table Talk*, published in New York in 1835, Americans regarded what was said of them in England 'a thousand times more than they do any thing said of them in any other country'.[62] Mill and other English commentators on the United States greeted such cultural deference with satisfaction, not untouched by a sense of intellectual superiority.

The English journalist and travel writer Edward Dicey, the brother of the jurist Albert Venn Dicey, reinforced such attitudes in his book *Six Months in the Federal States* (1863), which he dedicated to Mill.[63] Like other British visitors, he felt most comfortable in New England, with its strong links with the mother country and endearing Anglophilia. Bostonians, he observed, were avid readers of the latest English writings, familiar with the incidents of English life, and 'knew more about England than they did about America'. English critics, he added, who assumed that American was 'a hateful country' and its system of government 'repulsive' would find it strange on visiting Boston that the 'old love for England still crops out, in the almost touching cordiality with which an Englishman is welcomed here'.[64]

Leading Americans often seconded such views. The historian Henry Adams recalled his New England childhood in the mid-nineteenth century: 'the tone of Boston society was colonial. The true Bostonian always knelt in self-abasement before the majesty of English standards; far from concealing it as a weakness, he was proud of it as his strength.'[65] As Ralph Waldo Emerson remarked: 'The American is only the continuation of the English genius into new conditions, more or less propitious. See what books fill our libraries. Every book we read, every biography, play, or romance, in whatever form, is still English history and manners.'[66] An American historian observed that before the Civil War 'the longing for English praise, the submission to English literary judgment, the fear of English censure, and the base humility with which it was received, was dwelt on incessantly'.[67] But was American dependence on English culture consistent with patriotic claims to exceptionalism, and did it threaten to frustrate American democracy? As Mill saw it, the idea that America was a unique political experiment was unpersuasive given the ties of language, law and constitutional history. But the frustrations of American democracy had little, if anything, to do with Britain. Rather, they largely flowed from a want of education. A successful democracy required not only a dominant middle class paid decent wages, but also independence of thought and 'universal reading'.[68] In the United States, he remarked, 'there is no highly instructed class; no numerous body raised sufficiently above the common level, in education, knowledge, or refinement, to inspire the rest with any reverence for distinguished mental superiority, or any salutary sense of the insufficiency of their own wisdom'.[69] It was no surprise that people in the same social and economic circumstances thought alike, favoured the second rate, and were intolerant of the dissenting few. The very lack of classes defending their opinions against the majority was debilitating, leading to deference and adulation of the ruling power. In a democracy the natural tendency of people

will be to flatter the inclination towards substituting delegation for representation. All who have a bad cause will be anxious to carry it before the least discerning tribunal which can be found... and to persuade the many, that their own common sense is quite sufficient, and that the pretenders to superior wisdom are either dreamers or charlatans.[70]

As a man who admired Americans as a kindred people, who shared the same language and political traditions, Mill avoided the sort of insults made by other Englishmen, including Carlyle, who described Americans as 'eighteen Millions of the greatest *bores* ever seen in this world before'.[71] Nor did he equate a leisured elite with a spirited intellectual culture, for he recognized that art and literature could proliferate in a democracy without genius or social improvement. But, like Tocqueville, Mill complained of an absence of originality in literature, art, and philosophy that compromised American democracy. In his view, the United States required a learned class to leaven the tyranny of the philistine commercial interest. Indeed, learning was 'the great and salutary corrective of all the inconveniences to which democracy is liable'.[72]

Mill was a democrat who feared democracy, valued individualism, and wished to protect the elite from the tide of mediocrity. The best government was patently government by the wisest. The powerful current of anti-elitism in America, and its relative lack of a learned class, dimmed the prospects of a rational consensus based on clear thinking.[73] Americans sometimes mirrored such worries. In his Springfield speech of 1838, Lincoln had called passion America's 'enemy' and declared that the defence of the nation required 'cold, calculating, unimpassioned reason...moulded into *general intelligence*'.[74] Mill, who gave recurring expression to his fears about the threat democracy posed to the intellect, ended *On Liberty* (1859) with a famous line that echoed the fears of Tocqueville: 'A State which dwarfs its men, in order that they may be more docile instruments in its hands even for beneficial purposes—will find that with small men no great thing can really be accomplished.'[75]

Despite Mill's high opinion of *Democracy in America*, he thought the political experiment across the Atlantic too recent for anyone to comprehend its consequences fully. Though hesitant to pronounce on the future of the United States, Mill modified his views on freedom and representative government upon reading *Democracy in America*.[76] As he wrote in his *Autobiography* (1860): 'In that remarkable work, the excellences of Democracy were pointed out in a more conclusive, because a more specific manner than I had ever known them to be, even by the most enthusiastic democrats.' After reading Tocqueville, he added, 'my own thoughts moved more and more in the same channel, though the consequent modifications in my practical political creed were spread over many years'.[77] Thus, if only indirectly, the example of America was important in his political thinking and, by extension, to the development of British liberalism.

In his critique of *Democracy in America*, Mill said relatively little about the ins and outs of American politics. But he wrote to a friend in 1842 that he followed events in the United States, particularly the issue of slavery, 'very sedulously & interestedly'.[78] From time to time he commented on American affairs in print. In 1850, for example, he wrote a leading article on the California Constitution in the *Daily News*, in which he praised the document for prohibiting slavery and giving women the right to their own property.[79] Having digested Tocqueville's ideas, he eventually turned his mind to the dignity of the self-governed life in *On Liberty* and the virtues and defects of democracy in *Considerations on Representative Government* (1861). In the former book he skated over his views on government—and America—preferring to write a panegyric to the sovereignty of the individual.[80] In the latter book—a paean of praise to 'the ideal type of perfect government'—he updated his views on America, which he gave a mixed review.

In *Considerations on Representative Government* Mill returned to the theme that representative systems turned out second-rate candidates in elections, a tendency that the United States 'strikingly exemplified'.[81] It should be said that he was now writing against the background of a more highly developed party system and a succession of lacklustre presidents between Andrew Jackson and Abraham Lincoln. These uninspiring leaders were clearly in Mill's mind when he returned to the issue of American politics, which so often elected officials of little merit or experience. His belief in the need for effective American leadership had hardened because of the crisis of the Union. It was no longer plausible to argue, as he had done in his review of *Democracy in America*, that the United States did not require distinguished leaders because it was stable and enduring.

Mill believed that in America all selfish ambition gravitated towards the Demos. Consequently, the political parties never dared put forward their strongest, most experienced candidates because they had made themselves objectionable to some group of voters. To enter Congress it was a necessity to be a representative from a state in which you were a resident, subject to all the pettiness of local politics that went with it. Furthermore, the prizes of state politics were insufficiently grand to attract distinguished candidates. The consequence was that many of America's finest minds were alienated from national office 'as if they were under a formal disqualification'.[82] This compelled the majority to accept the weakest candidate or 'the worst of themselves'. While many Americans recognized these evils they had become inured to them, but at a serious cost to minority rights and to liberty:

> Now, nothing is more certain, than that the virtual blotting-out of the minority is no necessary or natural consequence of freedom; that, far from having any connexion with democracy, it is diametrically opposed to the first principle of democracy, representation in proportion to numbers. It is an essential part of democracy that minorities should be adequately represented. No real democracy, nothing but a false show of democracy, is possible without it.[83]

Mill, like Tocqueville, recognized the need for restraints on popular rule. He favoured democracy guided by eminent individuals and thus pressed for reform that would encourage the political participation of people of superior intellect and experience. Ideally, they would represent minority interests, enliven democracy, and check the despotism of the benighted majority. It was a theme that had occupied him in his earlier analysis of Tocqueville, but which was more urgent given the collapsing American Union, which the succession of unmemorable Presidents and Congressmen had failed to address. As things stood in America there existed a 'false democracy which, instead of giving representation to all, gives it only to the local majorities, the voice of the instructed minority may have no organs at all in the representative body'. In this faulty democratic system, the cultivated classes, certain of defeat, avoided running for office. As a consequence they became 'the servile mouth-pieces of their inferiors in knowledge'.[84]

Mill was of the opinion that institutions shaped the national character of a country and that they did so by their spirit rather than by their provisions. In a striking passage he chastised the very spirit of the revered foundation documents of the republic:

The American institutions have imprinted strongly on the American mind, that any one man (with a white skin) is as good as any other; and it is felt that this false creed is nearly connected with some of the more unfavourable points in American character. It is not a small mischief that the constitution of any country should sanction this creed; for the belief in it, whether express or tacit, is almost as detrimental to moral and intellectual excellence, as any effect which most forms of government can produce.[85]

It was not an opinion that was likely to endear Mill to those who saw the 'self-evident' truths of the Declaration of Independence as Holy Writ. While American liberals had long admired Mill, they gave *Considerations on Representative Government* a mixed review. It provided, as one scholar put it, 'philosophical utterance to the educative dimensions of democratic citizenship' that animated them, but Mill's desire to place checks on popular sovereignty was something of a stumbling block to American readers.[86]

Mill clearly had his doubts about the prospect of an improvement in the moral and intellectual capacity of the American public. He was not a child of the romantic movement, and with a mind formed by a secular outlook, he did not share Tocqueville's belief in the creative role of religion in shaping morality and sustaining the social order.[87] Rooted in a utilitarian tradition, he based his hopes for the future on rational argument and political reform rather than custom and the radical implications for personal identity in religious belief.[88] Tocqueville argued that 'one must maintain Christianity within the new democracies at all cost'.[89] Mill, whom Walter Bagehot placed in the 'unspiritual order of great thinkers', avoided the subject of religion in his critique of *Democracy in America*.[90] For him, Christianity and education were in tension, and he did not see religion as an engine of enlightened democracy.

Mill hoped to check the tyranny of the uninstructed by a graduated suffrage and the election of more progressive politicians. He endorsed a scheme, first proposed by Thomas Hare for the British electorate in 1857, whereby those who did not like the local candidates would be able to select from a national list of prominent men, with whose general principles they agreed.[91] This would open up the election to men of distinction, who, without local influence and party affiliation, stood no chance of being elected by the majority of any existing constituency. In this scheme, those voters who did not wish to be represented by local candidates would return a person they preferred among men across the country who wished to run for office. Thus the minority of educated minds scattered through the local constituencies would unite to return a number, proportioned to their own numbers, of the ablest men in the country.[92]

For Mill, the result would be to give reality to the electoral rights of the otherwise disfranchised minority and counter 'the natural tendency of representative government, as of modern civilization... towards collective mediocrity'. This tendency was increased by extensions of the franchise, which put the principal power in the hands of classes with lower levels of education, who were rarely interested in government. In America's 'false democracy', the voice of the instructed minority may have no say at all in the representative assemblies. While the reform he proposed would not give superior intellects a majority, it would at least guarantee that they would be heard. Sadly, Mill noted, such a scheme was unlikely to be adopted in America, where the majority was unenlightened and conformist. But had such a plan suggested itself to the framers of the American Constitution, 'the Federal and State Assemblies would have contained many of these distinguished men, and democracy would have been spared its greatest reproach and one of its formidable evils'.[93]

Nor was Mill content with the procedures for the election of the American President. 'A most important principle of good government in a popular constitution', he argued, 'is that no executive functionaries should be appointed by popular election: neither by the votes of the people themselves, nor by those of their representatives.'[94] While the American Presidency might be an exception to this general principle, the question was not without difficulty. He thought the indirect election by the Electoral College little more than a partisan charade, but he wondered whether it was a good idea to provide for the election of the President every four years in the first place. Mill saw some advantage in a stable country like the United States, where a *coup d'état* was unlikely, in making the executive independent of the legislature. It was in accord with the avoidance of great power in the same hands, which was desired by those who wrote the Constitution. 'But the advantage, in this instance, is purchased at a price above all reasonable estimate of its value.'[95]

For Mill there was much to be said for the British practice of appointing the chief minister from the representative body. 'In the first place, he is certain, when thus appointed, to be a more eminent man.' Typically, the majority in the British Parliament appointed it own leader, who was always one of the foremost people in political life. In contrast, 'the President of the United States, since the last survivor of the founders of the republic disappeared from the scene, is almost always either an obscure man, or one who has gained any reputation he may possess in some other field than politics'. The decline in the quality of presidents was not accidental, but the natural result of eminent men not standing as candidates. As Mill had observed before, prominent men created enemies and alienated some constituency, making them unelectable. And he added, perhaps with the recent election of Lincoln in mind, that obscure men without antecedents, of whom little is known, are readily elected.[96]

Another mischief Mill detected in the presidential system was the incessant electioneering. 'When the highest dignity of the State is to be conferred by popular election once in every few years, the whole intervening time is spent in what is virtually a canvass.' In America, the President and his party followers were all 'electioneerers', and the whole nation became preoccupied with personalities, while issues were discussed without reference to their merits. He did not acquit the Constitution, which had encouraged such mischief: 'If a system had been devised to make party spirit the ruling principle of action in all public affairs, and create an inducement not only to make every question a party question, but to raise questions for the purpose of founding parties upon them, it would have been difficult to contrive any means better adapted to the purpose.'[97]

The power of dissolving Parliament, which was a feature of British government, appealed to Mill because it eliminated the possibility of a political stalemate. As a principle, the executive should have the liberty to call for a new election when circumstances required it. When a President and Congress quarrelled, a deadlock could ensue that might last for years without resolution. To expect the executive and the Congress not to 'paralyse each other's operations, is to suppose that the political life of the country will always be pervaded by a spirit of mutual forbearance and compromise, imperturbable by the passions and excitements of the keenest party struggles'. Mill concluded that if the President, like a British Prime Minister, had the power to dissolve the Congress and appeal to the people it would give him greater independence from the legislature.[98]

Mill believed America had produced one of the few effective Federal unions in the world, though it was under extreme pressure when he was writing *Considerations on Representative Government*. (The book appeared in the same month as the opening battle of the Civil War at Fort Sumter.) He credited Hamilton, Madison, and Jay, the authors of the *Federalist*, for writing the most instructive treatise on Federal constitutions and for guiding the republic through a difficult transition. As in all representative governments, the American Constitution created a legislative branch and an executive; and while Mill was not generally in favour of second chambers he thought the provision in the American Constitution of providing an upper and lower house of Congress 'exceedingly judicious'.[99]

Mill admired the provision by which there were two Senators for each state, whether large or small, while each state elected Representatives in the ratio of the number of its inhabitants. This precluded any undue power from being exercised by the more powerful states and guaranteed the reserved rights of the state governments by making it difficult for any measure to pass Congress unless approved by a majority of voters as well as by a majority of states. Mill also approved of the indirect election of Senators by select bodies, which he believed raised the standard of qualifications in one of the legislative chambers. (Congress passed the 17th amendment that established the direct election of Senators in 1912.) Like most Englishmen, he preferred the Senate, which contained the more remarkable men in American public life, while dismissing the House of Representative as a chamber of museless nobodies.[100]

A principle Mill thought essential for the survival of an effective Federal government was that the central government should be granted the authority to make laws that citizens of every state had to obey. Without this power, no Federal mandates opposed by a local majority would ever be executed. Moreover, central government should have the power to execute the laws through its officers and enforce them through its tribunals. In successful federations every citizen owed obedience to two governments—his own state and that of the federation. This required that the constitutional limits of each authority be clearly defined and that the power to decide disputes should reside in an independent umpire. In the case of the United States this power resided in the Supreme Court.

In *Considerations on Representative Government*, Mill attributed many of the benefits of the justice system to a Supreme Court that did not declare the law in the abstract but waited until a case was brought before it. This had the effect of allowing the popular discussion to have taken place before a decision had to be made. Impartial justice was the goal and this required the intellectual pre-eminence of Supreme Court justices. 'There is nothing which more vitally imports the American people, than to guard with the most watchful solicitude against everything which has the remotest tendency to produce deterioration in the quality of this great national institution.'[101] Sadly, as Mill recognized, a Supreme Court of impartial, pre-eminent justices could not be guaranteed in a highly charged political atmosphere, as the Dred Scott case illustrated.

For Mill, the very stability of the justice system had been undermined by the Dred Scott decision (1857), which denied citizenship to those of African descent and held that Congress did not have the power to outlaw slavery in the Territories. The judgment, in his view, spelt disaster for the Union, for it threatened to topple the legal pillar of the Constitution.[102] As he saw it, Federal systems demanded mutual sympathy among the populations. In the United States, where conditions otherwise favoured a successful union, 'the sole drawback' was the issue of slavery, which threatened to disrupt a tie valuable to both sides. Mill was unusual in his day for his belief that observable differences in racial character were the result of the environment, which reinforced his view that slavery was the greatest blight on the American republic. He looked forward to the day when 'the opening words of the Declaration of Independence will cease to be a reproach to the nation founded by its authors'.[103]

The outbreak of the Civil War intensified Mill's interest in America. In 1862, he published two highly charged articles, 'The Contest in America', and 'The Slave Power', in which he attacked the British press for its indifference to slavery. Slavery was an offence against civilization, and he had little patience with his fellow countrymen who failed to see that the contest was a war against injustice. Initially, he doubted whether the North saw the struggle in those terms. 'But there was from the beginning, and now is, a large infusion of that element in it; and this is increasing, will increase, and if the war lasts, will in the end predominate.' Should that time come, he believed that mankind's greatest disgrace would receive its *coup de grâce*, and 'the Free States will have raised themselves to that elevated position in the scale of morality and dignity, which is derived from great sacrifices consciously made in a virtuous cause'.[104]

For Mill, the Civil War was a conflict with profound implications for democracy and humanity. For him, it was less about North and South than about 'free and slaveholding America'.[105] He rejoiced when he heard the news of Lincoln's desire to declare all states in the South free should the North win the war. He wrote to the American historian John Lothrop Motley in October 1862, two months before the Emancipation Proclamation, that no American read about President Lincoln's intention to abolish slavery 'with more exultation than I did'. Again, he apologized for British ambivalence over slavery and took the Tories to task for wishing to see the United States broken up. 'As long as there is a Tory party in England it will rejoice at everything which injures or discredits American institutions.' He was horrified that his fellow countrymen were making such a poor showing during the Civil War and was anxious that Americans should not think worse of them than merited.[106] Such views endeared him to Northern intellectuals at the same time that it bolstered the Union cause in Britain.[107]

Mill had been receptive to his friend Thomas Carlyle's ideas about the 'Great Man' in history, an individual who had an extraordinary impact on events; and Lincoln, though not an obvious great man at the time of his election, eventually filled the hero's shoes. (Lincoln had his own version of Carlyle's theory, in which he feared that an American

Caesar would appear whose ambition would destroy what the nation's founders had built.[108]) Mill was deeply impressed by Lincoln's handling of the war and his determination to end slavery. He wrote to the Irish economist John Elliot Cairnes that the President was 'a very favourable specimen of an American public man, and a credit to the nation which elected him, as he seems to be simply honest without any trick or charlatanerie'.[109] He replied to another correspondent who said that the President had overstepped the Constitution: 'I have always admired Lincoln, among other reasons, because even for so great an end as the abolition of slavery he did not set aside the Constitution but waited till he could bring what he wanted to do (by a little straining perhaps) within the license allowed by the Constitution for military necessities.'[110]

The abolition of slavery and the victory of the North in the Civil War erased many of the doubts about American democracy that had coloured Mill's earlier opinions, opinions that led one US reviewer of *Considerations on Representative Government* to call him 'a true son of John Bull'.[111] American reviewers, at least those from the North, would have been more flattering had they noticed Mill's about-face on America at the end of the Civil War. Mill had always preferred the traditions of the middle-class puritans of Boston to the aristocratic, slave-owning Virginians.[112] In a letter to a correspondent in 1865, he credited the courage and energy of New England's institutions and people with 'the immortal glory of having destroyed slavery'. He lamented that Tocqueville had not lived to see what the New England states have become: 'he would, I think, have acknowledged that much of the unfavourable part of his anticipations had not been realized. Democracy has been no leveller there, as to intellect and education, or respect for true personal superiority.'[113]

To Mill, the re-election of Lincoln was a great event; his assassination a dreadful shock: 'Lincoln is a glorious martyr if there ever was one', he wrote, 'he is not to be pitied—to be envied rather. One's feeling is all personal—it is as if a ruffianly assassin had deprived one of a dear personal friend.'[114] He did not think the cause would suffer, however, and might in fact gain from the indignation aroused. In a letter to Cairnes, Mill observed 'that the death of Lincoln, like that of Socrates, is a worthy end to a noble life, and puts the seal of universal remembrance upon his worth. He has now a place among the great names of history.'[115] Despite the loss of the President, he looked forward to a great future for America, 'provided that the North was not foolishly generous to its conquered enemies'.[116]

Mill had long criticized the United States for what he saw as its stagnant democracy and low morality, but Lincoln's political genius and the abolition of slavery renewed his faith in the American people. If he had found fault with the Constitution of 1787, he could not find fault with its progressive amendments in the 1860s. He even reconsidered American education, which had failed to impress him in the past. In a letter to a correspondent in the United States at the end of 1865, he praised Americans for the great benefit they had conferred upon mankind 'by showing what democracy and universal education together can do—how they make a whole people heroes when heroism is required, and peaceful citizens again as soon as the necessity is ended'.[117]

Mill continued to brood over the implications for European society of advancing democracy and declining aristocracy, but he found consolation in America, where he saw popular government showing signs of progress despite the turmoil and injustices of reconstruction. As for many other Englishman of his generation, the end of slavery reinvigorated his sense of the unity of Anglo-American culture, which had come under strain during the Civil War. The erstwhile provincials had earned a place in his esteem. In 1867, he described himself to Samuel Wood, a populist politician from Kansas, as 'one who takes as deep and continuous an interest in the political, moral and social progress of the United State as if he were himself an American citizen'.[118] But in 1869, for reasons of work and 'the shortness of life', he turned down the offer of a lecture tour of the United States from the American Social Science Association.[119] Thus Mill died without visiting a nation where he would have felt at home.

3

Walter Bagehot
The Tyranny of the Constitution

No one in England will be much impressed by any arguments which tacitly assume that the limited clauses of an old state-paper can provide for all coming cases, and for ever regulate the future.

(Walter Bagehot, 1861)

Success in a lottery is not argument for lotteries. What were the chances against a person of Lincoln's antecedents, elected as he was, proving to be what he was?

(Walter Bagehot, 1867)

Walter Bagehot has been called 'the greatest Victorian'.[1] He was born in Somerset in 1826, the only surviving child of a Unitarian banker, and educated at University College, London. Though called to the Bar in 1852, he returned to Somerset, and while working in his father's bank filled his idle hours writing biographical and literary studies. A judicious marriage to the eldest daughter of the owner of *The Economist* introduced him to the charms of a more cosmopolitan society and led to a dramatic change in his employment. In 1861, he returned to London where he became editor of the weekly. There he shifted his attention to economics, high politics, and constitutional issues. A brilliant polymath, he examined the lives of individuals and the machinery of government in a vivid, epigrammatic style that embellished a mind of great subtlety. The fate of free institutions fascinated him; and as a 'parliamentary historian' by temperament, he consequently applied his playful intelligence to the leading political drama of the day, the crisis of American democracy.[2]

Bagehot was the most gifted political writer of his generation in the English language, and his trenchant remarks on the American Constitution were wide-ranging reflections on the structure and practical effects of government. Like Burke, he distrusted theory and had a gift for seeing things in context. Both men saw the English Constitution as a source of useful political habits. But Bagehot did not share Burke's reverence for it as a cathedral of government built over the centuries by English genius. For him, history was 'not a source of prescriptive wisdom'.[3] The English Constitution was an ingenious 'hypocrisy' with an array of outmoded relics on the surface and an efficient modern machine below.[4] He took exception to the belief in constitutions as founts of eternal wisdom. Nor did he subscribe to what he called the 'historic twaddle about the rise of liberty', which may be seen as a comment on Tocqueville.[5] Such views set him apart from an established school of American authorities, who saw their Constitution as having a providential meaning, which set their nation on an inexorable march towards freedom.

Constitutionally, Bagehot was a sceptic. Indeed, scepticism was characteristic of Victorian writing about American government, which has had recurring British echoes ever since. 'An Englishman is generally amazed that the American constitution works at all', intoned *The Economist* in 1937, on the 150th anniversary of the signing of a draft Constitution for the United States in Philadelphia.[6] The opinion mirrored that of its former editor, who thought the dead weight of a written document, made sacred for want of a hereditary sovereign, an impediment to resilient, effective governance. The crucial issue was whether institutions worked, not whether they could be deduced from abstract principles.[7] To Bagehot, Americans had been duped by the outmoded doctrines of the Founding Fathers and the fossil erudition of the legal priesthood, which led to misconceptions with grave political consequences. No Englishman, he wrote, would be much impressed with arguments that assumed 'that the limited clauses of an old state-paper can provide for all coming cases, and for ever regulate the future'.[8]

Bagehot never visited the United States but nonetheless had strong views about its people, whom he described as impulsive, ill educated, and easily manipulated.[9] Like other Englishmen he was prone to see Americans through an English lens, in his case confusing them with the half-educated working men of Lancashire.[10] Still, he admired their energy, pluck, and respect for the law. He took these characteristics to be Anglo-Saxon, an appellation Englishmen were prone to use when admiring of their transatlantic cousins. As the tensions mounted between the Northern and Southern states, he took comfort from the assumption 'that Anglo-Saxon sense and Anglo-Saxon principles' would preserve Americans 'from the fate of Mexican and Spanish impulsiveness and imbecility'.[11] He was drawn to the United States because it was 'the greatest and best of presidential countries'.[12] Given America's Anglo-Saxon origins, it provided a worthy constitutional parallel to Britain, and a contrast between what Bagehot called its 'presidential system' and the 'cabinet system'.[13]

* * *

Though formally a liberal, Bagehot could not be called a democrat. He has been well described as a 'moderate Liberal' with conservative leanings.[14] He admired the pre-1832 electoral system, which offered a wide variety of franchises. A uniform franchise, in his view, was bound to rest on the uniformity of the lowest and swamp the upper-class vote.[15] Though opposed to universal suffrage, he was open to working-class representation if it could be achieved in a way that did not diminish the dominance of property owners. Bagehot was preoccupied in the 1860s with the spread of democracy to Britain's industrial cities, where impoverished wage earners without a stake in the economy were susceptible to agitators.[16] As a traditionalist mid-Victorian, he feared that if the democratic door opened, Britain would become 'a worse America, in which the lower orders are equally despotic, but are not equally intelligent'.[17]

Conservative instincts invigorated Bagehot's fondness for the upper classes and sustained his belief in a hierarchical conception of society, in which people knew their place in the social and political order. In an article in the *National Review* of 1859, he wrote that an individual had a right to 'so much political power as he can exercise without impeding any other person who would more fitly exercise such power'.[18] As he saw it, the democratic suffrage in America had led to vulgarity and ill-considered legislation. Moreover, egalitarian countries were 'fatal to that development of individual originality and greatness by which the past progress of the human race has been achieved, and from which alone, it would seem, all future progress is to be anticipated'.[19] The presumption that a society worked best when every one was on a level with every one else was, to Bagehot, an insult to social refinement and ambition. He favoured a system of 'removable inequalities'—a cliché among British patriots in the 1860s—by which members of the working class might raise themselves in the social scale through perseverance and the emulation of those above them.

The role of a leisured class was not simply to govern but to provide a theatrical show of pomp and trappings, at whose centre was the monarch. To Bagehot, concrete symbols represented general principles to the unsophisticated, who understood politics in terms of loyalty to individuals. A stable society was made up of elites who encouraged deference through spectacle and governed through symbol.[20] Like many educated Englishmen, Bagehot did not overrate the political capacity of the common people, though he admired their skills and ingenuity. The poor should have a voice, but he did not wish to hear it prevail in Parliament. In his view, the English working classes contributed little to public opinion, but he applauded their deference and 'stupidity', which was a source of social stability and countered troublesome theorizing. 'If you once permit the ignorant class to begin to rule you may bid farewell to deference for ever.'[21]

Turning to the United States, he noted that deference was not so deeply ingrained as it was in Britain. Despite their Anglo-Saxon origins, Bagehot thought Americans rather like the French—too impulsive and impatient to govern themselves. In his view, political ignorance was pervasive in the United States, but, unlike deferential Britain, the stupid could not be relied upon to see the merits of the wise. The central dilemma of democracy was how to get the ignorant majority to elect their educated betters. Constitutional devices were inadequate, for the voters were unlikely to adopt measures intended to limit their own powers. So too were panaceas like Hare's electoral scheme, promoted by Mill, which, in Bagehot's opinion, would simply encourage the corrupted party machines. If in Britain stupidity was a safeguard against theory, in America it was an impediment to good governance. A workable democracy required inducing the 'self-satisfied, stupid, mass of men to admit its own insufficiency'.[22]

* * *

Bagehot studied *Democracy in America*, but it is rarely mentioned in his writings, for he was more interested in the nitty-gritty of politics than in social theory. To his mind, the French had 'a morbid appetite' for logical deduction and theorizing, which had led to political instability and social upheaval.[23] Thus he was never likely to endorse the luxuriant speculations of Tocqueville, whom he met in 1857 at the London home of James Wilson, his future father-in-law.[24] Bagehot doubted the premise that democracy was inevitable and desirable, but he accepted that American trends were a portent of Europe's future, not least for Britain. In surveying the United States government, it was the tyranny of the Constitution that alarmed him more than Tocqueville's tyranny of the majority. The more he studied the American Constitution the more enamoured he became of Britain's unwritten one. For him, the sovereignty of an abstract, written document was harder to fathom than the sovereignty of a living monarch, who disguised the complexities of the British government.

Given his anxieties and interests a comparison between the British and American people and their Constitutions became a compelling theme in his political writings. The British Constitution was to Bagehot a marvel of intelligible government, which superimposed the poetry of monarchy upon the more doubtful benefits of a burgeoning democracy. It was subtly effective, created over centuries by a careless race that 'captured the imagination of the ignorant and satisfied the reason of the educated'.[25] However complex in ritual and administration, it was essentially simple: 'The action of a single will, the fiat of a single mind, are easy ideas; anybody can make them out, and no one can ever forget them.'[26] But for him it was its elasticity that made the English Constitution perennially relevant.

To Bagehot, the English Constitution was a mass of fictions that usefully disguised inconsistent practices.[27] It bore little resemblance to the descriptions of it in books. In contrast, he saw the American Constitution as a text in need of a new edition. Politics is not literature, and constitutions needed to keep pace with social change. The ancient, but malleable English Constitution did so seamlessly. It was, in Bagehot's metaphor, 'like an old man who still wears with attached fondness clothes in the fashion of his youth: what you see of him is the same; what you do not see is wholly altered'.[28] The withered body under the eighteenth-century apparel was all too apparent to him in the American Constitution, and he intended his writings to undress the rigid corpse.[29]

Article 5 of the Federal Constitution, which made amendment difficult, has been seen as a stroke of genius by many commentators, for it provided needed stability to an experimental government.[30] Bagehot saw the Article as the dead hand of the eighteenth century, undermining the normal development of the nation. Clearly, a Federal system that required three-fourths of the disparate states to ratify an amendment was contentious. The framers had been so fearful of placing sovereign power anywhere that they devised a system by which the Constitution could only be changed by authorities outside it. That a minority of small states could stifle the will of the majority was to Bagehot a defect that induced paralysis. In his opinion, the consequence of Article 5 was that obvious evils could not be remedied and that 'absurd fictions' had to be invented to get around the harmful clauses. 'The practical arguments and the legal disquisitions in America are often like those of trustees carrying out a misdrawn will—the sense of what they mean is good, but it can never be worked out fully or defended simply, so hampered is it by the old words of an odd testament.'[31]

* * *

Britain's Constitution favoured speed, America's favoured security.[32] Arguably, no system of government that divided power between legislative and executive branches had resolved the difficulty of combining decisiveness and safety. Bagehot believed the British cabinet system excelled in a concentration of effective power. Following the 1832 Reform Act, it had reached a stage where a decision could be made quickly but risked getting it wrong. The American presidential system provided safeguards against ill-considered legislation but risked delay. As every constitutional critic on either side of the Atlantic was aware, the most troublesome example of delay was over the issue of slavery, which had bedevilled the United States since the birth of the republic. The result was the Civil War, which Bagehot thought a more flexible Constitution would have prevented.

With the issue of slavery never far from his mind, Bagehot was robust in his condemnation of the divided sovereignty of the American government, which he thought unsuited to swift and effective action. One of his principal objections was that presidential and congressional terms were for fixed periods. The long hiatus between elections and inaugurations, which has often frustrated American voters, further exacerbated the problem. For their part, the British people could choose a new leader in a crisis, changing 'the pilot of the calm' for 'the pilot of the storm'. Since an election might be called at any moment the press and the voting public consequently paid close attention to the facts and debates and felt that their judgement had influence. As Bagehot noted, 'the *Times* has made many ministries'. The Washington newspapers, in contrast, 'can no more remove a president during his term of place than the *Times* can remove a lord mayor during his year of office'.[33]

The problem of delay in replacing an unpopular or incompetent President has often taxed the American public. One thinks of the paralysis of the James Buchanan administration before the Civil War, or, looking forward from Bagehot's day, one recalls George W. Bush idling out his term of office in the face of two wars, an economic crisis and the lowest popularity rating for a President in decades. A comparison of Roosevelt's election in 1932 with the formation of the Churchill government in 1940 is instructive. That the two men rose to their respective challenges suggests that both the British and American systems of government are capable of throwing up great leaders in a crisis. Yet the American public had to wait what to many seemed an eternity to replace the ineffective Herbert Hoover, whereas Churchill formed a government within weeks of a vote of no confidence in the Chamberlain government.

Although the British Constitution might strike many as absurd in theory, it was arguably efficient in operation, for it allowed shifts of opinion to change prime ministers without waiting for a fixed election. To Bagehot, America's Constitution was the reverse. It was inelastic in operation because it was inefficient by design. The President, though impeachable in theory, is virtually irremovable in practice. Moreover, the electorate, far removed from the lawmaking process, has little influence. Apart from the electing moment 'it has not the ballot-box before it; its virtue is gone, and it must wait till its instant of despotism again returns.'[34] (Rousseau had made a similar point about the British political system in the *Social Contract*.[35]) For Bagehot, a politics that made it virtually impossible to remove a president in 'a quick crisis' was folly, for 'the time when a sovereign power is most needed, you cannot *find* the supreme people'.[36] The election of an obscure 'village lawyer' in 1860 raised this very issue.

As a banker and financial journalist with an interest in fiscal policy and the cotton trade, Britain's commercial interest influenced Bagehot's thinking on American politics. Like many free-trade English Liberals, he had no particular fondness for the North and its high tariffs, nor for 'Yankee brag'. Like his Unitarian father, he was a man who hated slavery and had little sympathy for the South and its 'deeply ulcerated semblance of civilization'.[37] But it was the collapse of the Union that turned his mind to essential constitutional issues. The Civil War, he argued, threw 'an intense light on the working of a presidential government at the time when government is most important'.[38] Was the Constitution's elaborate machinery suited to the shifting requirements of a supreme crisis? Or did it exacerbate the crisis? What was the future of democracy in an era when the masses were in the ascendancy? Was Lincoln a likely saviour of the nation?[39] How was reconstruction to be successful in a nation that remained divided at the end of the Civil War?

Bagehot wrote nearly forty well-informed articles on America in the 1860s, in which he considered a host of issues, from slavery to British neutrality, from the Lancashire cotton famine to Abraham Lincoln. At the heart of his musings on American government was an analysis of what he described as the 'purely pernicious' defects in the Constitution.[40] 'It is impossible for Englishmen', he wrote in 1861, 'not to observe that the whole mischief has been, not *caused* but painfully exasperated by the unfortunate mixture of flexibility and inflexibility in the United States Constitution.'[41] He singled out for blame the peculiarity in the American government of having a President elected for a set term but largely independent of the confidence of the Congress. He was convinced that the slave states would not have reacted so violently, or unanimously, if a congressional defeat could have given them relief, as a parliamentary defeat did in England.[42]

Bagehot admired undivided administrative power. For him, a cardinal failing of the American government was that it lacked the simplicity of a single sovereign authority, which the House of Commons provided in Britain. The American system, in his mind, was unwieldy, founded on a mistaken interpretation of the English Constitution current in the eighteenth century, the theory of the separation of powers.[43] As other English critics noted in the 1860s, the US system of government was so carefully poised that any disturbance in the political machinery stopped it working, without a defined authority to deal with unexpected events.[44] To Bagehot, the framers of the Constitution had created a system of ingenious devices, 'the most complicated which could well be imagined', which simply 'aggravated the calamities of their descendents'.[45] They had created paper checks and balances and competing branches of government to ensure that the state did not degenerate into tyranny. But to Bagehot, such a system simply slowed down the process of government, made it more difficult to organize public opinion, and, most damagingly, erected barriers between the executive and the legislature.

Bagehot disapproved of Federal systems with their dual demands of unity and independence, and in the American case he took particular exception to the states acting as rivals of central government. Consequently, he much admired Alexander Hamilton, whom he described as 'the greatest political philosopher' among the framers of the Constitution.[46] He regretted that Hamilton's plans for a 'general government' could not be achieved, but accepted that the Founding Fathers had little choice but to cave in to the local suspicions of the states at the expense of national efficiency. The resulting compromise was a Federal Union in which each state was a subordinate republic and in 'some sense a centre of disunion', a state of affairs that was only likely to succeed in 'circumstances exceptionally favourable'.[47] To make matters worse, the part of authority given to the Federal government was itself divided and subdivided: 'All Federal government is, in truth, a case in which what I have called the dignified elements of government do not coincide with the serviceable elements'.[48] Tellingly, he used the word 'serviceable' in describing Congress rather than 'efficient', which he used to describe the House of Commons.

That the American President reigned largely independent of Congress alarmed Bagehot, for it isolated the executive from congressional influence and made him far more personally responsible for policies that needed occasional modification. Unlike the British Prime Minister in a cabinet government, the President did not share responsibility with his parliament nor have to defend his policies before it. Congress, in Bagehot's view, was wholly unfit to make executive decisions and thus left everything to the President: 'But what is really wanted for the effective administration of a free country in times of excitement, is that the government should be in such connection with the people as to direct the national policy in harmony with their gradually forming convictions. For this purpose, the ruler must himself belong to the representative body.'[49]

Bagehot understated the role of Congress in shaping legislation, and he underestimated the prestige of the Senate, which, unlike the House of Representatives, was a semi-permanent body with only a third of its members having to run for office every two years through indirect elections.[50] But he had a point in his observation that the separation of the executive and legislative branches, which the Founding Fathers thought essential to a good government, had serious repercussions. The exclusion of ministers from Congress resulted in cabinet officers being deprived of parliamentary careers. More often than not cabinet officers served the President without previous political experience and without political prospects. As he saw it, the lack of a political training for administrative leaders led to the degeneration of public life, a view widely shared by other British commentators, including Mill, who thought parliamentary government better suited to producing effective statesmen.

Nor did the separation of powers enliven congressional legislators, who, isolated from the executive, tended to resentment and antagonism. Their debates and votes could not depose an executive and, as Bagehot put it, were thus 'prologues without a play'. To belong to a debating society hanging on to the coat tails of a President was unlikely to 'stir a noble ambition' and encouraged inactivity: 'The members of a parliament excluded from office can never be comparable, much less equal, to those of a parliament not excluded from office. The presidential government, by its nature, divides political life into two halves, an executive half and a legislative half; and, by so dividing it, makes neither half worth a man having.'[51] To Bagehot, the Civil War demonstrated this defect in the American government with devastating results.

* * *

As *The Times* of London observed in 1862, the American crisis was emphatically 'the battle of a constitution', in which there was no self-interpreting power that could decide which reading was correct.[52] Clearly, there was a momentous flaw in the instrument itself, for at the time of its framing the Founding Fathers disagreed as to its meaning and spirit, and the issue of slavery had been glossed over by compromise. When it was suggested that a written Constitution presented the potentially dangerous consequences of rival interpretations, the framers assumed that the Supreme Court could settle all difficulties with its irresistible authority. This was wishful thinking to Bagehot, who was less enamoured of the American judicial system than Tocqueville or Mill. In his view, the granting of Petrine power to judges was misguided, for when a contentious issue erupted no court could resolve an extra-judicial matter beyond its competence.[53] To a man of his persuasion, the Dred Scott case was an unhappy reminder of the fallibility of judges, who had tenure for life in the Supreme Court.

Before the Civil War, Bagehot doubted that the North could win a contest with the South, and argued that Americans should not oppose the severance of the Union as long as it could be achieved without civil bloodshed and slave insurrection. At that time he was positive about the prospects for the North, both in its foreign and domestic affairs, if the Union collapsed: 'The same energy and enterprise which have made them so great in spite of the difficulties of a slave connection will carry them on still faster and further when liberated from this hampering incubus.' Should an independent Southern state emerge, he assumed that it would continue to carry out a flourishing trade with Britain and the North but that the underground railroad would 'work faster than ever'. He predicted a worsening of relations between the races in the South with 'no daylight through this appalling picture'.[54]

Soon after the outbreak of the Civil War, Bagehot wrote an essay in the *National Review* titled 'The American Constitution at the Present Crisis'. He praised the document for protecting property and fostering commerce, which made America a nation to watch. But it contained the seeds of national dissolution, for America's stability depended on the voluntary union of the states. That the nation had survived its inherent contradictions surprised him. He dismissed the notion that the Constitution was a fit instrument to resolve differences of opinion over slavery. In his view it was born in a time of confusion, framed by a pressing necessity between 'two extreme plans for meeting that necessity'.[55] An Englishman, he remarked, knows that all written documents 'will fail utterly when applied to a state of things different from any which its authors ever imagined'.[56]

The Civil War broadened Bagehot's interests from constitutional issues to a consideration of the wider political culture, which he found wanting in America. Like Mill, he believed rationality and the diffusion of education necessary in raising the standards of American government.[57] It was an unhappy prospect that progress depended on stifling diversity in an age of mass politics.[58] Increasingly, he was sensitive to what he saw as the evils of Jacksonian democracy, which had encouraged the greater political participation of the common man. In expanding the American electorate 'the Constitution had become an almost unmitigated *ochlocracy*', in which the 'half educated' masses were 'everywhere omnipotent'. Americans were an untried people in his view, whose moral fibre was in doubt in a crisis. (He attributed their success in the Revolution to the 'indescribable imbecility' of the British.) The institutions of eighteenth-century America were free but not democratic. But since Washington's time, men of 'noble sentiments and stainless honour' had retired from the scene, giving way 'to dirtier and rougher men' in tune with mass democracy.[59]

Bagehot felt comfortable with America's aristocratic traditions, and like most British commentators looking back on the early years of the republic he was sympathetic to the Federalists, who represented the educated classes and favoured a strong central government. The growing political power of the great unwashed alarmed him, for it exposed the nation to the whims and passions of the ill-educated masses. Moreover, it compounded the Constitution's failure to address the divisions between the states. 'The existing crisis in America', he observed, 'had been intensified almost as much by the precautions which the original founders of the Constitution took to ward off what they well knew to be the characteristic evils of democracy, as by those evils themselves.' He lamented America's 'vulgarity' that troubled so many cultivated Europeans, and he observed, in a telling sentence, that should the American Union fall, it would be 'little regretted by those whose race is akin, whose language is identical, whose weightiest opinions are on most subjects the same as theirs'.[60]

Bagehot shared the general view in Europe that the government of the United States was ineffectual and that its leaders had 'degenerated frightfully'.[61] He had read Mill's *Considerations on Representative Government* before he published many of his own writings on America, and it appears to have influenced his thinking on an electoral system that had been corrupted by the rise of party politics. Like Mill, he thought the process by which Americans chose their leaders prevented men of talent and experience from rising to high office. In contrast, the candidates propelled by the British electoral system were household names, indeed 'household ideas'. The unhappy history of the United States under the lacklustre President Buchanan suggested to him that it was 'a singular defect in the working of the American

Constitution that it gave power at the decisive moment to those least likely to use that power well'.[62]

To Bagehot, the rot started in the American primary campaigns, in which few cared little whether a man was fit for the job, preferring to dwell on his attractiveness as a candidate. He blamed the Constitution as much as the voting public. The framers were anxious to avoid momentary gusts of popular opinion but desired that the President be widely representative. Accordingly, they created the 'farce' of a 'double election', in the hope that the Electoral College would exercise discretion and provide a check on popular ignorance. The effect, in Bagehot's mind—and to many other critics—was to create futile complications that turned out to be woefully at odds with the Constitution's original design. 'In reality, the "Electoral College" exercises no choice: every member of it is selected by the primitive constituency *because* he will vote for a certain presidential candidate…and he does nothing but vote accordingly.'[63]

In a nation split into disparate sections, each with its peculiar enmities and traditions, rivalry for the presidency becomes intense. It was a necessity for national politicians also to be state politicians. As Mill and others had pointed out, the consequent involvement in the petty squabbles of local legislatures deterred talented men from entering public life. Bagehot believed that men running for office in such circumstances were bound to have said something that would offend some large constituency. As a result, presidential elections could only be secured after long deliberation. In practice, each party caucus selected the most unexceptionable member available, typically a trimmer with little talent and commonplace views. 'If a man of wit had devised a system specially adapted to bring to the head of affairs an incompetent man at a pressing crisis, it could not have devised one more fit.'[64]

This was the system that elected Lincoln, which, given the gravity of the unfolding crisis, placed him in the most invidious position ever experienced by an American politician. The 'spoils system', the practice of dismissing the Civil Service on a change of government, only worsened matters. The Civil War expanded its possibilities.[65] Bagehot thought it foolhardy that at the very moment when the state was collapsing, the President had to spend his precious energy turning out the friends of his predecessor and appointing friends of his administration. Bowed down by the minutiae of office, he had 'the detestable necessity of deciding on the respective fitness of five thousand men for five hundred postmasters' places'. In an emergency, the President should be able to concentrate on more serious concerns and 'to call to his aid a popular assembly, animated by all the feelings which a great crisis calls forth in a great people'.[66]

But Congress was elected years before when no such crisis existed, made up of men, many of them sworn enemies of the administration, who had different priorities. Given the division of powers in a nation collapsing into Civil War, Congress was useless as a partner and dangerous as an opponent. To Bagehot the moral was plain:

> The Constitution of the United States was framed upon a vicious principle. The framers were anxious to resist the force of democracy—to control its fury and restrain its outbursts.... They hoped to control the democracy by paper checks and constitutional devices. The history we have sketched evinces the result; it shows that these checks have produced unanticipated, incalculable, and fatal evil, but have not attained the beneficial end for which they were selected. They may have ruined the Union, but they have not controlled the democracy.[67]

* * *

Initially, Bagehot, like Mill, saw President Lincoln as the type of man who tended to emerge under the defective electoral system created by the Constitution. In June 1861, only months into Lincoln's first term, Bagehot wrote that the President was

> a nearly unknown man—who has been little heard of—who has had little experience—who may have nerve and judgement, or may not have them—whose character, both moral and intellectual, is an unknown quantity—who must from his previous life and defective education, be wanting in the liberal acquirements and mental training which are the principal elements of an enlarged statesmanship.[68]

Some years later, he observed that the notion of elevating

> a man of unknown smallness at a crisis of unknown greatness is to our minds ludicrous. Mr Lincoln, it is true, happened to be a man, if not of eminent ability, yet of eminent justness.... But success in a lottery is not argument for lotteries. What were the chances against a person of Lincoln's antecedents, elected as he was, proving to be what he was?[69]

Bagehot dismissed the President as a nonentity at the beginning of the Civil War, and during the conflict criticized him for mismanaging it. He took particular exception to the suspension of *habeas corpus*, which the Constitution did not authorize Lincoln to set aside. Bagehot accepted that in a crisis of imminent danger to the public the executive may exercise powers that normally did not come with the office, but doing so amounted to the 'entire suspension of all civil rights and liberties throughout the *states* by the arbitrary fiat of the *Federal* Government'. He did not see the necessity of the writ and fully expected the citizenry to resist it: 'If Mr Lincoln endeavours to enforce his decree, the tyranny will exasperate many of his Northern supporters. If he recalls it, the weakness displayed in the whole transaction will disgust them even more.'[70]

Nor did Bagehot approve of Lincoln's Proclamation emancipating the slaves. Unlike Mill, who praised the measure, he thought it 'injudicious' because it would create dissension, paralyse action, and prolong the war. Indeed, he described the proclamation as so half-hearted and inconsistent that it would alienate Europeans, who were running out of sympathy for the North. What was the point, he noted, of Lincoln proclaiming the emancipation of slaves whom he could not free, while retaining in slavery those whose fate lay within his power? 'The position taken by the President in this decree is so curiously infelicitous, so grotesquely illogical, so transparently *un*-anti-slavery, that we cannot conceive how it could have emanated from a shrewd man and have been countersigned by an educated one.'[71]

For all his criticisms of Lincoln during the war, Bagehot came to revere him by the end of it. As he put it 1865: 'Power and responsibility visibly widened his [Lincoln's] mind and elevated his character.'[72] Underlying Bagehot's constitutional views there was more than a trace of Carlyle's 'Great Man' theory, and Lincoln had become one through his handling of the war. In his admiration for the hero in history, Bagehot shared the opinion of Mill and others of his generation. But the President's achievement came as something of a surprise to both men, for they assumed that the American political culture discouraged men of talent, leaving the field to untested hacks. That Lincoln rose to the occasion was the exception that proved the rule.

Bagehot thought the President's assassination arguably the most significant event since Waterloo. Just when Lincoln's character and genius gave both North and South hopes of reconciliation, a Southern murderer gave occasion for a further outbreak of sectional hatred and diminished the prospects of reconstruction:

It is not merely that a great man has passed away, but he has disappeared at the very time when his special greatness seemed almost essential to the world, when his death would work the widest conceivable evil, when the chance of replacing him, even partially, approached nearest to zero, and he has been removed in the very way which almost alone among causes of death could have doubled the political injury entailed by the decease itself. His death destroys one of the strongest guarantees for continued peace between his country and the external world.[73]

Unlike Mill, who believed Lincoln's assassination might be used to advance the liberal cause, Bagehot was more pessimistic about the future of the United States without exceptional leadership and a reformed Constitution. To heal the wounds of the Civil War, it was essential that central government be strong, for he believed that if it was weak it was likely to be violent.[74] The difficulty for America was that there were so many barriers to strong government in a system with divided sovereignty. The Civil War, as he saw it, was a battle over Federal power, and he hoped that the Northern victory would give a deathblow to the doctrine of states' rights, which the Constitution enshrined. If it did not, fruitless contests between the centre and the periphery would continue to damage the country.

Bagehot forgave Lincoln's 'despotism' because he managed to establish a strong central government. He thought the problems faced by the President were multiple, the natural result of a defective political system. First, the abstract dislike of America's Federal government had reached the level of 'a quasi philosophical theory'. Secondly, the Constitution created a Federal system deliberately calculated to frustrate the exercise of central power. Thirdly, the Constitution had 'the moral weight of a religious document' and was thus virtually impossible to alter.[75] Whether the document is difficult to amend because of the reverence in which it is held or because Article 5 puts such a burden on anyone seeking to alter it is open to dispute. But to Bagehot, the combination of public sentiment, states' rights, and Constitutional dogma meant that government was rarely able to act decisively.

For Bagehot, weak presidencies were the natural result of a defective Constitution, which was, as critics recognized, drafted before the formation of political parties in America. It took a President of political genius to overcome the imperfections of the very Constitution to which he swore an oath. For Bagehot, the need for presidential genius only confirmed that the 'limited clauses of an old state-paper' were neither adequate nor decisive in a crisis. As the Civil War suggested, effective change may require a benevolent monarch creating and tapping a shifting public mood and testing the limits of the Constitution. This was Bagehot's view of Lincoln's political wizardry during the Civil War. Happily for the United States, President Lincoln proved so consummate a politician that he provided a cure for the constipation of American politics. The President was that unique executive, who, Bagehot claimed, was 'so shrewd that he can steer his way amidst the legal difficulties piled deliberately in his path, and so good that he desires power only for the national ends'. Lincoln combined such a degree of sagacity and sympathy that he attained a 'vast moral authority' that made 'the hundred wheels of the Constitution move in one direction without exerting any physical force'.[76] In Lincoln, Bagehot found his ideal American ruler, an enlightened despot whose 'dictatorship' the extreme circumstances of the day excused: 'We do not know in history such an example of the growth of a ruler in wisdom as was exhibited by Mr Lincoln.... A good but benevolent temporary despotism, wielded by a wise man, was the very instrument the wisest would have desired for the United States.'[77]

For Bagehot, Lincoln was an enlightened, uncrowned monarch. Indeed, he described the presidency as 'an unhereditary substitute' for a king in *The English Constitution*.[78] It is a curious feature of the American presidential system that while born out of revolution it still closely resembles that of England in 1776, with an executive cum head of state—reminiscent of King George III—who is treated with much of the reverence that attends a sovereign. Meanwhile, the British political system moved on, mixing constitutional monarchy and parliamentary government, with a ceremonial head of state separated from the executive Prime Minister. While the American President is now often regarded as 'imperial', the British Prime Minister is now often regarded as an 'elected' monarch, but without the ceremonial trappings that enlarge the presidency and shield it from the derision dished out in a parliamentary system.[79]

As the historian Jacques Barzun observed, Bagehot was a 'Socratic ironist in politics'.[80] Clearly, he had a propensity to 'an abstracting cleverness'.[81] In keeping with his intellectual nimbleness, Bagehot argued that in Britain a republic had 'insinuated itself beneath the folds of a Monarchy'.[82] His view of Lincoln as a benign despot suggests that he, like a host of other British writers, believed the American Constitution created an elective monarchy that had insinuated itself beneath the folds of a republic. He would have seconded William Seward, who told a London journalist while serving as Lincoln's Secretary of State that 'we elect a king for four years, and give him absolute power within certain limits, which after all he can interpret for himself'.[83] Given Bagehot's respect for deference and authority, the expansion of presidential power in the Lincoln administration—some have called it abuse of power— was a feature of American government of which he approved.

Bagehot's belief that the United States was a disguised monarchy was gaining currency in the mid-nineteenth century because of expanding executive authority, which the Constitution did little to allay and under Article 2 much to promote. American historians have largely ignored the monarchical elements in the Constitution, which several of the Founders endorsed, though rarely with frankness.[84] At the end of the eighteenth century John Adams, for example, called the United States 'a monarchical republic'.[85] Attributing kingly powers to America's highest office is a recurring theme in United States history, though the idea makes Americans uncomfortable. But to Bagehot, the notion appealed to his sense of irony and his belief in the malleability of constitutional language, if not a belief in the malleability of the American Constitution.

* * *

Bagehot was not one to favour easy innovation. What he famously called 'the cake of custom' in *Physics and Politics* should be sufficiently stiff to make political reform difficult, but not so stiff as to prevent durable progress.[86] In his view, the Founding Fathers had overcooked the Constitution. For all their genius, they had been unwise to encumber the nation with an unyielding form of government difficult to amend, which led to civil strife, political inertia, and legal dissension. In his mind, constitutions were not simply about legality, stability, and authority, but also about flexibility, form, and aesthetics. The American Constitution appeared inelegant to a man who disliked Federal systems with their divided sovereignty and intrinsic rivalries. Furthermore, the authority that was reserved for the Federal government itself created a divided, inefficient system in which 'the Congress rules the law and the President rules the administration'.[87] Bagehot, a latter-day champion of Hamilton's lost cause, admired structural coherence in government under a unified authority, which is why he saw such beauty in the biddable English Constitution. Constitutional rigidity, in Bagehot's opinion, sapped America's vitality and left it unresponsive in an emergency. The results were all too apparent to him when he wrote *The English Constitution*. The end of the Civil War was a critical juncture in American history. The South lay at the feet of its Northern conquerors who had to decide the fate of the secessionists. The former slaves remained at the mercy of the 'mean whites', whom Bagehot described as 'perhaps the most degraded, ignorant, brutal, drunken, and violent class that ever swarmed in a civilised country'.[88] As he saw it, such monumental issues created a political crisis and the greatest moral challenge to the United States: how to change former foes into friends. 'But there is no decision, and no possibility of a decision. The President wants one course, and has power to prevent any other; the Congress wants another course, and has the power to prevent any other. The splitting of sovereignty into many parts amounts to there being no sovereign.'[89]

The abruptness and finality that marked the end of the Civil War shocked Bagehot, like many other European commentators.[90] A dividedness of mind pervaded his writings throughout the conflict, not untouched by his concerns for British commerce. Despite the prolonged upheaval, he anticipated little disruption to future trade and prices between America and Britain. While he saluted the 'vanquished gallantry' of the Confederates, he felt a personal sympathy with the Northerners. 'They have won, as an Englishman would have won, by obstinacy.'[91] Before the outbreak of the war he saw merit in a two-state solution. At the end of it, he would have been content to see the collapse of the Union and the emergence of an independent South, as long as it did not resuscitate slavery.

While Bagehot was sanguine about the North, he fully expected the South to remain chaotic for the foreseeable future, and assumed 'that it must pass through a social revolution'.[92] He would have wished it to pass through a constitutional revolution as well, though the assassination of Lincoln and the timidity of the Johnson administration made this unlikely. His line of argument suggests that the post-war crisis would have been an opportunity to establish another Constitutional Convention to rethink the electoral system and relationship between the Federal and State governments. What he failed to credit was that the Federal Constitution, for all its failings and evasions, had proved flexible enough to survive the challenge of secession.[93] Instead of the document coming in for revision, Americans, having persuaded themselves of its providential genius, continued to rally to its banner.

The Civil War had brought out Bagehot's prejudices along with his passions. At the end of it, he took heart that slavery was at an end, but for a man given to the practical effects of politics, he saw problems ahead more clearly than many of his contemporaries. Unlike Mill, who might be accused of wishful thinking about reconstruction, Bagehot was quickly disillusioned. He feared the task was fraught with difficulty. The Northern victors had to deal with a dissolved Southern society and had to perform the task of reform with a defective Constitution and through the instrumentality of men who were hostile and sinister in their designs. He believed the Southerners would be successful in evading the full results of their admission that slavery was over by indirect measures that were 'insidious, oppressive and unwise'.[94]

His sympathy for the 'unhappy negroes' was palpable. In 1865, he laid out his feelings in one great, impassioned sentence:

Liberated from their old masters and unable to find new ones for themselves,—helpless with the helplessness natural to men who have never been taught or allowed to initiate or arrange their own actions, and not knowing how to set about any work which is not prepared for them, but calling for the most part in vain, because their liberators, with the best will in the world, simply cannot provide sustenance or organise employment for such vast and sudden numbers,—little inclined to labour at all, as might be expected, because labour in their minds is associated with slavery and liberty with idleness,—despised and not loved (to say the least) by the great mass of the Northerners and actually detested by the Irish,—hated at once with mortification of defeat and the bitterness of destitution, by those to whom they were a short time ago both slaves and wealth,—and exposed, therefore on all sides to ill-treatment and neglect against which, and the consequences of which, nothing short of ubiquitous omnipotence could effectually protect four millions of suddenly emancipated serfs,—these unhappy victims of philanthropy and civil war are dying, we are told, by thousands; numbers are shot on the slightest provocation or from sheer brutality by the miscellaneous ruffians who abound there; numbers more sink under disease and famine; numbers emigrate northward, to fare no better; the law does not protect them; the civil authorities will not; the military authorities cannot.[95]

* * *

In an essay in *The Economist* of 1867, 'The Contending Policies in the United States', Bagehot came back to his central theme about

American government: the pernicious effects of its Constitution. The outdated document that was woefully inapplicable to a post-war Union divided into bitterly opposed castes. Looking back, he saw the Civil War as a 'Secession War', a revolt of the Southern states against Federal power, and he clearly missed Lincoln's centralizing tendencies.[96] Only a strong central government could deal with the deficiencies of an unreformed Constitution and combat the post-war residue of embittered and ignorant Southerners bent on keeping freed slaves in bondage. On these grounds, he proposed a military occupation in the South to maintain order and to protect those institutions capable of administering impartial justice and educating former slaves.[97]

Bagehot worried lest President Johnson prove yet another political non-entity. He felt that the office of Vice President, which the framers of the Constitution wished to fill with the 'second wisest man' in the state, had collapsed into a sinecure filled by obscure men selected to ensure party unity.[98] His 'interim' view was that President Johnson was 'very like an average Scotch tradesman, very shrewd, very pushing, very narrow, and very obstinate, inclined to take the advice of any one with more *knowledge* than himself, but unable to act on it when opposed to certain central convictions'.[99] He castigated the President for his 'superstitious' contention that the Union had never been divided and therefore declined to build new legislation on this 'absurd and unreal a figment'. The machinery of an effective Constitution only worked in unified societies and America remained divided. President Johnson's folly was to have made an 'idol of the Constitution' and to ignore facts that were 'irreconcilable with the legal construction of this particular document'.[100]

To Bagehot, the Constitution had not prevented a war and it was irrational to expect it to prevent further conflict after it had so been defied. Indeed, he accused President Johnson of welcoming further destruction if it derived from the legitimacy of the Constitution. He concluded that those radicals who did criticize the Constitution fell back on the Declaration of Independence, 'and try to get out of that great aboriginal document of their history what they fail to extract from the organic structure of their government. In the Declaration that all men are born free and equal, they imagine that they have a supplement to the Constitution, and one in which they can find a cure for their recent troubles.'[101] Americans, to Bagehot, were the victims of their reverence for imperfect documents that were political expedients designed for the infant republic. Instead of a malleable Constitution designed for a changing society, America required its citizens to conform to an antiquated state-paper. Still, at the end of the Civil War, Bagehot, like Mill, applauded Americans for letting daylight in on the Constitution by the abolition of slavery and praised them for giving sway to Lincoln. The Northern victory in the Civil War and the end of slavery had shown American democracy to better effect than he might have imagined when he first turned his attention to the United States. While he continued to decry the rigidity of the Constitution, he took particular pleasure in the Fifteenth Amendment, which entrusted the vote to former slaves, who helped to re-elect President Grant in 1872.[102] For all his criticisms of America's inability to resolve its post-war crisis, he paid tribute to 'Anglo-Saxon' Americans for rising from time to time above their inflexible Constitution: 'If they had not a genius for politics; if they had not a moderation of action singularly curious where superficial speech is so violent; if they had not a regard for law, such as no great people have yet evinced, and infinitely surpassing ours,—the multiplicity of authorities in the American Constitution would long ago have brought it to a bad end.'[103]

* * *

Bagehot continued to take a keen interest in the politics of the United States in the years after the Civil War. The impeachment of President Johnson in 1868 left a strong impression, confirming his belief that stalemate and rigidity were ingrained features of American government. The incident was conclusive proof against the Constitution as a Constitution: 'A hostile legislature and a hostile executive were so tied together, that the legislature tried, and tried in vain, to rid itself of the executive by accusing it of illegal practices. The legislature was so afraid of the President's legal power, that it unfairly accused him of acting beyond the law.' At the same time, he praised the political character of Americans during the crisis, for 'few nations, perhaps scarcely any nation, could have borne such a trial so easily and so perfectly'.[104]

Bagehot followed American elections closely and in 1876 wrote an essay in *The Economist* titled 'The Lessons of the Presidential Election'. In his view, the exact result of the contested election that brought

Rutherford B. Hayes to the White House would probably never be known but would be disbelieved by one half of the electorate, who could plausibly argue that corrupt officials manipulated the vote. He saw Hayes and Samuel Tilden as interchangeable candidates—the sort typically thrown up by the corrupted electoral system—but he applauded the patience and good sense of Americans who would cope with whatever harm resulted from the unhappy episode. 'Theirs is not a country in which, as the saying is, "the worst comes to the worst". If we may be excused for the apparent bull, in the United States the worst is very apt to come to the better.'[105]

Bagehot had long thought that the election of a President by the discredited machinery of the Electoral College was a political evil inflicted on the American people. And he could not resist the opportunity provided by the presidential election of 1876 to take yet another swipe at the American Constitution. A 'capital defect' of the electoral system fashioned by the document was its tendency to degrade politics rather than to elevate them. (This was a point others would make after the contested election of 2000, which brought George Bush to the presidency.) The fact that what would be more injurious in other countries was less injurious in the United States was, to Bagehot, no excuse for overlooking its debilitating effects: 'For if this great people can make so much of what has so many serious faults in it as the American Constitution, what might they not have made of a Constitution in which all those faults had been remedied.'[106]

Now armed with compelling evidence, Bagehot argued that the results of the constitutional regulations that created the Electoral College led to legal and moral doubts about the validity of presidential elections. Such uncertainty was itself 'a vulgarising element tending to discredit the great national act which has just been performed'. Only a very sober people would quietly endure not knowing whether the man they elected was indeed the man chosen to the nation's pre-eminent office. Bagehot recognized that political institutions could not work without a good deal of blind belief, and he understood that Americans had a deep conviction that their Constitution was divinely inspired for their especial purpose. Consequently, they disliked experiments that lay outside the document. But for his part, 'the sooner... an amendment to the Constitution, providing a better mode of election for the future, is considered or adopted, the better it will be for the American people'.[107]

* * *

After the trauma of the Civil War and the assassination of Lincoln, patriotic flag waving was rather less evident among Americans, making them more susceptible to criticism from abroad. But unlike other leading British commentators, Bagehot confined most of his views on the US Constitution to articles in English periodicals, which limited his readership. While American reviewers considered *The English Constitution* 'weighty' and 'well considered', they did not think it altogether just.[108] His literary and biographical essays had greater appeal in the United States. In 1891, an American corporation, the Traveler's Insurance Company, issued the first collected works of Bagehot in five volumes and sent copies to their policy holders.[109] Both his literary and political writings were a major influence on Woodrow Wilson, whose *Congressional Government* (1885) was a pivotal study of American politics. 'To ask your friend to know Bagehot is like inviting him to seek pleasure', he observed.[110] Wilson probably did more than anyone to enhance Bagehot's reputation in America. Sadly, the two men never met, for Bagehot died in 1877, at the inconsiderate age of 51, when Wilson was still a Princeton undergraduate. Decades later, the President would lay a wreath on the grave of the sage of his youth.

Bagehot's sardonic criticism of what Americans held most sacred was never likely to endear him to a mass audience. His writings on American politics and society, as opposed to his literary and biographical essays, had relatively little appeal in the United States beyond the academy, though they reinforced the existing prejudices of many of his English readers. He never visited the United States and thus his opinions on American culture drew heavily on caricatures of the country in Victorian travel writing, along with the more mournful predictions of Tocqueville. Consequently, his social analysis lacked the acumen of his constitutional analysis. He dismissed the 'low vulgarity' of its people but without ever moving among them. He studied the material facts of the country but had little feeling for the idealism of its citizenry. He admired America's enterprise and economic potential, but failed to see the quality and promise of its life. He stands accused by one of his biographers of misjudging 'the nature of American life, mistaking political democracy for a dead level of social mediocrity'.[111]

Still, Bagehot's critique of American government still resonates after a century and a half, if only because the Constitution is there, largely unchanged. But it was unduly severe, seen through a parliamentary lens, shaped by the exceptional circumstances of the Civil War and tinged by smugness about America that was typical of educated Englishmen of the day. Since his writings there have been, for better or worse, increasingly powerful presidents who have tested the constitutional constraints on the executive. There have also been numerous constitutional amendments, but they have not altered the complex, competitive structure of American government nor reformed the Electoral College. Bagehot complained that political and social change was more difficult to achieve in America than in Britain because of competing sovereignties and an intractable Constitution. But as a man wary of democracy and political innovation, he might have regretted the effects of a malleable, more easily amendable US Constitution.

Perhaps not surprisingly, this 'greatest Victorian' remains perplexing to American constitutional writers, who, with a few notable exceptions like Wilson, have chosen to ignore him rather than wrestle with his genius. Though an intellectual gadfly, Bagehot took pains over his writings on the US government, which may be seen as a tribute to an Anglo-Saxon constitutional tradition, which he, like other Englishmen, found both fascinating and disturbing in its American guise. As the most brilliant constitutional writer of his generation on either side of the Atlantic, he presents a challenge to modern-day advocates of the 'Strict Constructionist' school, who, should they read his musings on American government, may be unsettled by his scathing indictment of their beloved document. But whether the rival priesthoods translate the Constitution with literal exactitude or loose construction, the strictures of Bagehot are worth revisiting.

4

Sir Henry Maine
Democracy Denied

> We are propelled by an irresistible force on a definite path towards an unavoidable end—towards Democracy—as towards Death.
> (Sir Henry Maine, 1885)

> While the British Constitution has been insensibly transforming itself into a popular government surrounded on all sides by difficulties, the American Federal Constitution has proved that, nearly a century ago, several expedients were discovered by which some of those difficulties may be greatly mitigated and some altogether overcome.
> (Sir Henry Maine, 1885)

The English jurist and historian Sir Henry Sumner Maine might seem an unlikely advocate of the United States. A philosophical Tory with a deep dislike of democracy, he was nonetheless an admirer of the American Constitution. If Bagehot complained that effective governance was more difficult to achieve in the United States because of competing sovereignties and an intractable Constitution, Maine applauded the Constitution for impeding mass democracy. In his opinion, the great achievement of the Founding Fathers was their creation of institutional checks and balances, which obstructed majority rule and slowed down legislation. Like Mill, Bagehot and other Victorian political commentators, he saw the Constitution of the United States as an outgrowth of the British Constitution, but he had greater confidence in the American model because he believed it to be less malleable and consequently more conservative. The historian Thomas Babington Macaulay famously observed that the American Constitution was 'all sail and no anchor'.[1] Maine thought the reverse.

Maine was born in 1822, the son of a physician.[2] He was educated at Christ's Hospital in London and then entered Cambridge where he excelled as a prize-winning scholar. An American who knew him at Cambridge pointed to what was to become a feature of Maine's writing: he 'corrected mistakes in a way that one was not apt to forget'.[3] In an academic career that can only be described as spectacular, he moved from being a classics tutor at Trinity Hall to the Regius Professorship of Civil Law at Cambridge at the age of 25. (He was elected Master of Trinity Hall in 1877.) Though an ill-paid sinecure at the time, the Regius Professorship gave Maine the opportunity to reshape the law curriculum, giving emphasis to historical and comparative methods that linked legal scholarship with other branches of knowledge.[4]

In the following years Maine was called to the Bar and started work on what was to be his magnum opus, *Ancient Law* (1861), which transformed the study of jurisprudence and legal history. Its object, as he put it, was 'to indicate some of the earliest ideas of mankind, as they are reflected in Ancient Law, and to point out the relation of those ideas to modern thought'.[5] The book's central thesis was that law and society developed 'from status to contract'. In other words, in the ancient world individuals were bound by status to families and traditional groups; in the modern world they were autonomous agents who made contracts with whomever they chose. It was an original line of thought derived from serious historical scholarship, and it propelled Maine's reputation. As his biographer George Feaver observed, 'Maine's generation of lawyers and historians, from the first appearance of *Ancient Law*, viewed it with the same sort of enthusiasm as natural scientists had received Darwin's *Origin of Species*.'[6] Among the book's admirers was Bagehot, whose chief theoretical work *Physics and Politics* (1872) took inspiration from Maine.[7]

While Maine's reputation among legal historians and sociologists remains high, his reputation as a political theorist has waned, though there are signs that it may be gaining currency after a century of neglect, at least among American conservatives.[8] His essential political book *Popular Government* appeared in 1885. It was a collection of four related essays, significantly revised, that had been published in the *Quarterly Review* in 1883–4. The chapter titles of the book remained those of the essays: 'The Prospects of Popular Government'; 'The Nature of Democracy'; 'The Age of Progress'; and 'The Constitution of the United States'. In the preface he tells the reader that he had attempted in *Ancient Law* 'to apply the so-called Historical Method of inquiry to the private laws and institutions of Mankind'. *Popular Government* was to be the political sequel, in which he applied 'the Historical Method to the political institutions of men'.[9] It was arguably the most damning critique of democracy in the nineteenth century.[10]

* * *

Constitutional reform in Britain left Maine despondent and searching for a viable government that was free from what he saw as the democratic excesses in Britain. The United States was a fount of possibility, and Maine sought fortification against democratic advance. He found it in America. In much of his writing one can detect a nineteenth-century incarnation of Burke, who favoured a political system in correspondence to the hierarchical way of the world.[11] Unlike Tocqueville or Mill, who treated democracy broadly to incorporate society and political culture, Maine's chief concern was to retard the popular legislative will, which led him to concentrate more narrowly on political and institutional issues. For him the American Constitution was a historical treatise whose conservative principles might profitably be applied to British politics.

Over the years Maine had grown increasingly conservative, and by the 1880s thought that Britain was in a headlong rush into the perilous sea of experimental reform. Though its principles were drawn from Britain, America offered a striking contrast because its Constitution provided safeguards against reforming legislation, most importantly the reform of government itself. Change was a synonym for loss to Maine. To his delight, he discovered that constitutional change needed special sanction in the United States, and he urged his readers to learn a history lesson from across the Atlantic, where an eighteenth-century Constitution gave steadiness to a political system under tremendous pressure from economic and social transformation.

Maine was something of a rarity, at least to the modern American mind, for his conservative philosophy was based on history not religion and values. The historical record led Maine to suspect human nature and to oppose legislation, which he believed to be a harmful characteristic of modern democracy. As the British jurist Albert Venn Dicey noted: 'it is no mere accident that Maine, who in his *Ancient Law* undermined the authority of analytical jurisprudence, aimed in his *Popular Government* a blow at the foundations of Benthamite faith in democracy'.[12] If the phrase 'from status to contract' captured the essence of *Ancient Law*, the phrase 'from democracy to tyranny' might be said to do the same for *Popular Government*. Democracy, Maine argued, was only 'a form of government', albeit an extreme form, not an attitude of mind; and if unchecked, would ultimately move from its triumphant phase to a sullen despotism or the familiar refuge in Caesarism. In a striking sentence, his gloom unbound, he declared: 'We are propelled by an irresistible force on a definite path towards an unavoidable end—towards Democracy—as towards Death.'[13]

History furnished a guide to human progress to liberal historians like Lord Acton and George Bancroft, but to Maine it served as warning about democracy's frailty, which led him to a 'melancholy conservatism'.[14] Like many of his generation he was haunted by the turmoil of the French Revolution and the Napoleonic Wars, while his study of the ancient world made him wary of change: 'All things have happened already; nothing much came of them before; and nothing much can be expected of them now.'[15] The many years Maine spent in India where he served as a Legal Member of the Indian Council, may have reinforced such a philosophy. More certainly, his experience as a lawyer compounded his conservatism, for lawyers do not readily welcome legal change by inept legislatures, preferring the traditional wisdom of their profession. This was a chief reason for his aversion to change and specifically to democracy, which was the form of government most favourable to change.[16]

Maine professed not to know what progress meant to the liberal mind, but believed it had much to do with Rousseau, whom he disliked both for his views on the origins of society and for his recklessly democratic vision of politics. In *Ancient Law*, he had used the history of legal development to castigate Rousseau and other radicals, whom he pilloried as fantasists.[17] In *Popular Government*, he attacked them for making assumptions about political institutions unknown to history. Rousseau came under especial attack for his historical fictions and his belief in the omnipotent democratic state rooted in natural right. Maine abhorred first principles such as the 'General Will', which he found historically baseless. Rousseau's analysis of how communities formed was a chimera: 'the despotic sovereign of the *Contrat Social*, the all-powerful community, is an inverted copy of the King of France.... The mass of natural rights absorbed by the sovereign community through the Social Compact is, again, nothing more than the old divine right of kings in a new dress.'[18]

But Maine had a more pressing, political reason for opposing what he saw as Rousseau's a priori imaginings, for he believed that First Chambers in Europe had come under the influence of the *Social Contract*. They claimed to represent the will of the people and assumed 'an air of divinity which, if it rightfully belonged to them, would be fatal to all argument for a Second Chamber'.[19] Maine's politics turned on maintaining powerful Second Chambers, like the House of Lords and the American Senate, which did not represent the will of the people so much as what British Whigs called the 'best opinion'. Second Chambers added security and challenged the presumption that First Chambers were infallible. 'The conception of an Upper House as a mere revising body, trusted with the privilege of dotting i's and crossing t's in measures sent up by the other Chamber, seems to me as irrational as it is poor.' To Maine, the only truly successful institution established since the onset of modern democracy was a second chamber, the American Senate.[20]

Jeremy Bentham, the great advocate of legislative reform, also came under attack in *Popular Government*, as he had in *Ancient Law*. Maine thought Bentham was insensitive to history and consequently overestimated the intelligence of mankind. This led him to assume that men would use power in their own interest. Maine dissented: 'applying this rule to the whole of a political community, we ought to have a perfect system of government; but, taking it in connection with the fact that multitudes include too much ignorance to be capable of understanding their interest, it furnishes the principal argument against Democracy'. In his pessimistic polity, influenced by Machiavelli and Hobbes, democracy was the most difficult form of government, and this accounted for its ephemeral duration in the past. And the most fundamental difficulty of democracy lay 'deep in the constitution of human nature'.[21] Maine's faith in his fellow man, according to an American critic, was so slight that he saw the practice of democracy as the equivalent 'of intrusting a baby with a hammer and looking glass as a means of inculcating prudence and self-control'.[22]

For Maine, an exertion of will determined acts of government. 'But in what sense can a multitude exercise volition?' Enthusiasts for democracy simply exposed their shallowness by resorting to meaningless phrases such as the will of the people or public opinion. They made a fundamental mistake in mixing up 'the theory, that the Demos is capable of volition, with the fact, that it is capable of adopting the opinions of one man or of a limited number of men, and of founding directions to its instruments upon them'.[23] In his historical analysis Maine detected an American movement, not unlike the radical cause in Britain, determined to promote unrestrained democracy. The party system that established itself in the young republic exacerbated the problem by promoting factionalism and, in the Jackson administration, the principle of 'to the victors the spoils', which was a corrupting influence on politics.

There was much in Maine's analysis of America that resembled Tocqueville's tyranny of the majority and Mill's tyranny of conformity. There was also an undisguised disdain for the capacity of the common man, which exceeded even Bagehot's. Since democracy aimed at levelling and gave free rein to the censoriousness of ill-educated voters, it was often intolerant of individual and social distinction. But in practice popular governments are peculiarly open to the *tyranny of minorities*.[24] Maine understood this tendency and would have been content had the minority been a hereditary aristocracy. For him, the common man was the hero's backside, someone susceptible to manipulation by crank minorities that popular government encouraged. As he put it: 'A number of persons, often a small minority, obtain the ear of the governing part of the community, and persuade it to force the entire community to conform itself to their ideas.'[25] In America, this minority could turn out to be constituents from states with small populations, who, under the influence of political demagogues, held considerable sway in a Federal system.

As the American states extended the vote to all white men in the first half of the nineteenth century, the electorate sought to take public affairs into their own hands. But to Maine, the growth of the population and an expanding electorate led to a 'dead level of commonplace views', while compounding the opportunity for corruption. Like Bagehot, he believed that the primitive mind could only understand loyalty to a person. Weak minds yield to wilful ones. The ignorant masses, intolerant and reluctant to change their habits, only formed an opinion by following the opinion of somebody else. Whether the superior was a party leader or a newspaper editor, he was always a wire puller, the activist in modern popular governments who fanned the party flames and whipped the partisans into a frenzy. To Maine, nothing was more sinister in a democracy than the caucus, the stump, the campaign newspaper, the various means by which the wire puller and the artful phrasemaker appropriated to themselves 'the will of the people'.[26]

As a political theorist, Maine was something of a social psychologist.[27] He described the demagogic party hero as an artless stranger to truth, who could never be fair to his opponents or bold except in the interest of his partisans. The parties themselves had affinities with religion, and the party faithful, like sectarians, were 'apt to substitute the fiction that they have adopted it upon mature deliberation for the fact that they were born into it or stumbled into it'. Party discipline was essentially military discipline, which reminded Maine of mankind's primitive combativeness. Where party strife prevailed 'a great part of ordinary morality is unquestionably suspended; a number of maxims are received, which are not those of religion or ethics; and men do acts which, except as between enemies, and except between political opponents, would be very generally classed as either immoralities or sins'.[28]

Such effective devices infected all parties, making them more and more alike, while the resulting policy reflected those ideas most likely to receive the clamorous support of the majority. The wider the electoral base, the greater the likelihood of unintelligent legislation. The consequence was a polity 'growing ever more confused and capricious, and giving results even more ambiguous or inarticulate, as the numbers to be consulted are multiplied'.[29] In the end, according to Maine, popular government led to a mischievous ideology that failed to listen to rational, scientific arguments that ran counter to its prejudices. Radicals assumed that the extended suffrage would work in their interests, but they were deluded in thinking democracy progressive. Rather, it was fatal to the very progress they desired. Like Aristotle, Maine believed democracies were self-destructive and ended in dictatorship.[30]

While Maine thought Europeans wilfully ignored such trends, he credited America, despite its unsavoury politics, with at least addressing the issue of how to make democracy safe and workable. The remedies of Mill—plural voting and the representation of minorities—left him unmoved. Nor did he hold out much hope for civic engagement, for in his opinion the benighted public was incapable of effective action. Far from having elevating moral and educational effects, participatory democracy simply exacerbated the problems. Since the masses were vulgar, their participation could only lead to political indecency.

Only a minority were fit to govern; the majority should defer. Despite his pessimism and low view of human nature, Maine concluded that America had shown that democracy could be made tolerable by wise constitutional provisions thought out in advance.[31]

One of Maine's admonitions was that democratic politics, though exciting as a game, tended to excessive legislating by parties primarily intent on keeping their rivals out of power. In his view, it was impossible to have a flood of legislation that was both safe and beneficial. Happily, the American Constitution put roadblocks in the way. Maine delighted in paradox, and it was his hope that the oldest monarchy in Europe, after providing the principles on which the freest republic in the world were founded, received back from the organic law of that republic lessons in conservative wisdom that she sorely needed in her misguided experiment with democracy.[32] Americans often believed that the politics of the New World would come to the rescue of the Old, but not in quite the way Maine proposed. *Popular Government*, for all its praise of the United States, was bound to disconcert progressive Americans who assumed they were in the vanguard of democracy.

Looking over history, Maine concluded that enthusiasm for change was not only rare but also very modern, and he doubted that the movement towards democracy would lead to advance, if only because of public superstition. On the political front, he thought it mistaken to assume that popular governments were legislating governments in the past. 'An absolute intolerance... of change which in modern language we call political thus characterises much the largest part of the human race, and has characterised the whole of it during the largest part of its history.'[33] Maine believed man a creature of habit and that modes of conduct and behaviour were resistant to change; when men did alter their habits they did so with reluctance and pain. Of all the races, he conceded, the Anglo-Saxons were the most susceptible to changing their habits, which may be seen as a rare criticism of the English from a Victorian.

Maine took a particularly conservative view of the attitudes of women, whom he treated, like many a conservative clubman, as ornamental creatures whose lives were given over to morality and fashion. He confirmed that females had no desire for change by reference to the novels of Thackeray and Trollope! In a discursive aside, which could only irritate progressives, he described women as 'the strictest conservators of usage and the sternest censors of departure from accepted rules of morals, manners, and fashions'.[34] He applauded their constancy and resistance to politics, a line of thought that suggested that he did not much mix with the bluestockings of Somerville or Girton. Such opinions did not alarm the English and American reviewers of *Popular Government*, but they would have appalled Mill and Harriet Taylor had they been alive.

* * *

Reviewers in the United States treated *Popular Government* with the respect due a famous author, despite its pessimism and partisanship. They were hesitant to castigate a scholar of such distinction who wrote so favourably about the Founding Fathers and the US Constitution.[35] But some, ever sensitive to British opinion, thought he would have benefited from an American tour and that his judgement was biased by historical studies rather than practical experience.[36] Others, though happy enough with his praise of the Constitution, preferred Tocqueville's more invigorating *Democracy in America*.[37] Others still felt that applause from a man of Maine's politics was 'like praise of a play by a Puritan, or of a Protestant theological treatise by a Jesuit Father. The Constitution which makes democracy seem "tolerable" to a Tory is indeed a remarkable instrument.'[38]

Judging from the tone of the notices, *Popular Government* caused a greater stir in Britain, where it was seen as a political touchstone. (It went through six English editions between 1885 and 1910.) While conservatives thought it one of Maine's finest works, liberals took it to be a thinly disguised attack on Gladstone's policies. Matthew Arnold, who was just back from a tour of the United States, admired the chapter on the American Constitution but thought the book too legalistic.[39] The liberal historian Lord Acton, a friend of Maine's who had commented on *Popular Government* before its publication, called it 'A Manual of Unacknowledged Conservatism'.[40] John Morley, the editor and Liberal politician, compared passages of *Popular Government* to 'the drone of a dowager in the Faubourg Saint-Germain'. He described the book as 'a rattling Tory pamphlet under the disguise of philosophy', while 'the tone is that of the political valetudinarian, watching with uneasy eye the ways of rude health'.[41] Maine was known to be a cold, withdrawn personality in delicate health but with a brain and nerves always on the verge of 'morbid excitability'.[42]

Like other British writers on comparative government, Maine wrote with his fellow countrymen in mind and hoped that *Popular Government* would have an influence on British politics. It did not. While the book joined the canon of conservative texts, its impact was negligible, partly because it was querulous, partly because Englishmen were resistant to calls for the Americanization of their institutions, and partly because it was out of touch with democratic trends. Where Maine saw these trends as a sign of moral decay and political folly, the number of those who saw them as progressive and inevitable was growing. In an increasingly egalitarian era, the idea that 'where there is political Liberty, there can be no Equality' was not a winning rallying cry.[43] Moreover, it would have been naive to expect widespread support from members of the general public, whom he mocked as so uninformed that they did not recognize their own self-interest.

While *Popular Government* was notable for its historical breadth, it should be seen against the more immediate background of British domestic and imperial politics in the 1880s.[44] If that decade saw America in expansive mood, the mood in Britain might be described as troubled. As an avid imperialist, Maine had been growing increasingly alarmed over challenges to the exercise of British power in India, which he linked with worrying trends at home.[45] The rapid growth of unions and working-class self-consciousness, which led to the growing calls for greater state intervention in social and economic policy, were distasteful to a man who believed in limited government guided by an aristocratic elite. The balance of the country was changing as commercial and industrial wealth now bulked larger than the agricultural wealth of landowners. Maine was deeply unhappy when the third Reform Act passed in 1884. Though it stopped short of universal manhood suffrage, it gave the vote to agricultural workers and dramatically altered the structure of county politics, leaving Conservatives in disarray; the following year the Redistribution Act doomed the political power of the aristocracy.

To Maine, democrats skated on thin ice; aristocrats walked on terra firma. He wished to sustain the power of the landed aristocracy on cultural and political grounds. Like Mill and Bagehot, he admired the political talents of the upper classes and feared the rule of the numerical majority. To him, the possession of great estates implied greater administrative ability and kindlier relations between the classes than were likely in a plutocracy. Under all systems of government, whether aristocratic, democratic, or monarchical, it was pure luck whether the individual called to direct public affairs was qualified; but the chance of his competence was far greater under an aristocratic system than a democratic one. One of democracy's chief drawbacks was that, 'while it gives birth to despotism with the greatest facility, it does not seem to be capable of producing aristocracy, though from that form of political and social ascendancy all improvement has hitherto sprung'.[46] American democracy may not have produced a hereditary aristocracy on the British model, but its dynastic political families would serve as a substitute of sorts.

* * *

According to Maine, the American Constitution was 'much the most important political instrument of modern times'.[47] It not only exercised an influence on the forms of government in Europe but also did credit to republics, which had been in disrepute in the years before the emergence of the United States. America had little choice but to become a republic since hereditary monarchy was not an option. Republic, however, was a notoriously imprecise term—John Adams said the word was 'unintelligible'—and had been used for all manner of governments, including Britain's limited monarchy.[48] The framers of the Constitution wished to distance America from the turbulence associated with the ancient republics and to redefine popular government. In Maine's opinion, they dreaded chaos more than anything else and thus sought to create a modern republic that was 'saved from disorder by representative institutions'.[49]

Maine admired the *Federalist* but noted that the essays paid scant attention to the political experience of Britain. The framers of the Constitution had been subjects of the Crown and while they fought a war to get rid of George III and the British parliament, they had no quarrel with kings or parliaments. They needed to persuade the public, and an appeal to the politics of the mother county would have provoked resistance. Thus they disguised the British Constitution's influence on their thinking by reference to Montesquieu, who gave it to them indirectly. It was part of Maine's purpose in *Popular Government* to show that, despite the paucity of references to the British government by Hamilton, Madison, and Jay, the American Constitution was 'coloured throughout by political ideas of British origin, and that it is in reality a version of the British Constitution, as it must have presented itself to an observer in the second half of the last century'.[50] The linkage was an important issue to him because if American politics was seen as deeply indebted to Britain, then Britain might be more welcoming to American precedents in turn.

Maine observed that the British Constitution up to the Reform Act of 1884 was not only exceptional, but widely considered 'the envy of the world'. Since it had lasted for a long time other popular governments might last elsewhere. But only one nation consisting of Englishmen—the United States—had practised a modification of the British Constitution with success and that amidst material abundance. Like other British commentators, Maine applauded the distinctive Anglo-Saxon political culture that he saw as being uniquely suited to producing a stable democracy. 'It is not too much to say, that the only evidence worth mentioning for the duration of popular government is to be found in the success of the British Constitution during two centuries under special conditions, and in the success of the American Constitution during one century under conditions still more peculiar and more unlikely to recur.'[51]

Maine was at pains to persuade his fellow Anglo-Saxons in the United States that their Constitution, while forged from local materials, emerged out of the British past, not least its monarchical traditions. In his evolutionary doctrine, the modern state, with distinctively defined administrative departments, grew up under monarchical institutions. Indeed, monarchy was the forerunner of democracy. Maine defined democracy as 'inverted monarchy', a description that in his view answered to the historical process by which modern republics emerged. Thus, successive French republics were in this analysis 'nothing but the later French Monarchy, upside down'. Likewise, the American republic followed the same pattern. The Constitution and the legal system of the United States 'would be wholly unintelligible to anybody who did not know that the ancestors of the Anglo-Americans had once lived under a King'.[52]

Radicals, in Maine's view, made a mistake in believing that democracy and monarchy differed in essence. Democracy, after all, had the same conditions to satisfy, the same duties to discharge, and the same tests of success as monarchy. It was likewise a mistake to assume, as Tocqueville had done, that democracy was inevitable. Such an idea was of recent vintage and did not accord with the historical record, in which democracies had rarely preserved the national existence or attained national grandeur. To Maine, they were typically weak and turbulent and consequently ephemeral. Historically, monarchies had been tenacious and democracies fragile. For centuries, kingship was all but universal. The fathers of the American republic recognized these truths and 'over and over again betray their regret that the only government which it was possible for them to establish was one which promised so little stability'.[53]

What distinguished modern democracies was their desire to produce reforming legislation. By contrast, ancient democracies rarely legislated and put up nearly insuperable barriers to legal and constitutional change. To Maine, Americans had hedged themselves round in exactly the same way because they assumed that human happiness flowed from private energy rather than public legislation. Consequently they only passed laws 'within the limits of their Constitutions, and especially of the Federal Constitution; and, judged by what has become the English standard, their legislation within these limits is almost trivial'.[54] He applauded the 'legislative infertility' of the American democracy, for it controlled the anti-scientific prejudices of the listless and vulgar populace, who tended to make impossible demands in the name of freedom.

Maine was not one to see the United States as a beacon of freedom that demanded reverence. He took particular exception to the great booster of liberal reform in America, the historian George Bancroft, whom he mocked for indulging in rhapsodic figures of speech in praise of democracy.[55] The words and metaphors typically associated with democracy—freedom, revolution, and popular sovereignty—left him livid. While Maine thought the framers of the American Constitution sagacious, he did not see the formation of the document, in the words of Bancroft, as 'the most cheering act in the political history of mankind'.[56] Rather, it was a compromise that 'filled up the interstices left by the inapplicability of certain of the then existing British institutions to the emancipated colonies'.[57] To Maine, Bancroft's notion that democracy was the rising light that 'flashed joy through the darkest centuries' was claptrap.[58]

The forms of government that Maine most admired were aristocracy and constitutional kingship, which in his view encouraged compromise and provided more stability than modern democracies. Still, he found the United States companionable, despite its experiment with universal manhood suffrage. One of the things he most admired was how the American Constitution safeguarded freedom of contract, which gave protection to industrial and commercial property.[59] The success of American political institutions appeared to Maine to be the result of curbing popular impulses rather than giving rein to them. The contrast with Britain was never far from his mind. 'While the British Constitution has been insensibly transforming itself into a popular government surrounded on all sides by difficulties, the American Federal Constitution has proved that, nearly a century ago, several expedients were discovered by which some of these difficulties may be greatly mitigated and some altogether overcome.'[60]

Although Maine believed that no foreigner but an Englishman could understand the Constitution of the United States, he was anxious to dispel some of the misconceptions about America that were abroad in Europe.[61] To do so he examined the Constitution of the United States in detail. He teased those who supposed the document 'sprang at once from the brain like the Goddess of Wisdom, an idea very much in harmony with modern Continental fancies respecting the origin of Democracy'. In keeping with his Burkean conception of the organic development of society, he believed the birth of the American republic was natural and flowed from ordinary historical antecedents. Where the Constitution was wise, it was in the skill of sagacious men who were conscious of inherited weaknesses that New World circumstances aggravated. The genius of the framers of the Constitution lay in their producing mechanisms calculated to minimize those weaknesses.[62]

Maine started with the presidency. When the framers of the Constitution looked for a substitute for the Crown, what they knew about government was the example of kingship. As Maine saw it, 'the resemblance of the President of the United States to the European King, and especially to the King of Great Britain is too obvious to mistake'.[63] While the framers of the American Constitution insisted on the differences between the presidency and kingship—the limited tenure and participation of the Senate in the exercise of power—they nonetheless took George III as their model. To Maine, Article 2 of the Constitution, which invested executive power in the President and gave him power over treaties and appointments, was convincing proof of elective monarchy in the making.

There was nothing very original in Maine's analysis of the monarchical nature of the presidency. The evidence was there for those who wished to find it. Maine knew that Hamilton and Adams wished to incorporate monarchical elements in the Constitution and that the contested office of the President had come under attack as an instrument of monarchy. The records showed that Patrick Henry saw the presidency 'squinting' towards monarchy.[64] His fellow Virginian, Governor Edmund Randolph, who attended the Constitutional Convention, regarded a unitary executive as 'the foetus of monarchy'.[65] From the earliest days of the republic, critics of presidential power had dubbed George Washington the 'monarch of Mount Vernon' and ridiculed President John Adams for his princely style.[66] The reigning Stadtholder of the Netherlands in the 1780s, William V, was among the Europeans who saw the President as an uncrowned monarch. As he said to Adams: 'Sir, you have given yourselves a king under the title of president.'[67]

In the 1830s, Americans had become increasingly sensitive to the growth of executive power in Washington—President Jackson appeared in a cartoon with a crown on his head and a veto in his hand.[68] The fear of an impending American monarchy was much in the news in the 1830s and 1840s. The Whig Party under the leadership of Henry Clay warned that 'the vast accumulation of executive power, actual and meditated' was leading towards 'an elective monarchy'.[69] Such views even reached the White House. In his inaugural address in 1841, President William Henry Harrison, who died of pneumonia soon after assuming office, reminded his audience that many of the framers of the Constitution opposed the extensive powers granted to the executive branch, and he lamented that American politics had for some years been moving towards a 'virtual monarchy'.[70]

It is likely that American worries about the emergence of elective monarchy had reached Maine. If not, he would have been aware of Bagehot's appraisal of the presidency as a substitute for a hereditary king in *The English Constitution*. And he probably had seen the oft-repeated remark of his contemporary Goldwin Smith, the eminent Oxford historian: 'the government of the United States is an elective monarchy; the government of England is a crowned republic'.[71] What Maine added to the discussion was a more elaborate analysis of the role of the executive in Britain and America. It began with a reference to the relative decline of the British monarchy, which gave him pause:

If Hamilton had lived a hundred years later, his comparison of the President with the King would have turned on very different points. He must have conceded that the Republican functionary was much the more powerful of the two. He must have noted that the royal veto on legislation, not thought in 1789 to be quite lost, was irrevocably gone. He must have observed that the powers, which the President shared with the Senate, had been altogether taken away from the King. The King could make neither war nor treaty; he could appoint neither Ambassador nor Judge; he could not even name his own ministers. He could do no executive act. All these powers had gone over to Mr Bagehot's Committee of Parliament. But a century ago the only real and essential difference between the Presidential and the Royal office was that the first was not hereditary.[72]

While Maine conceded that the presidential succession was not copied from Britain, he did not believe that the method of election had 'suddenly evolved from the brain of American statesmen'. First, the President, though elected for only four years, was to be indefinitely re-eligible. Thus the Constitution, though later amended on this point, did not preclude the emergence of an elective monarch for life, at least in theory, a point often lost on Americans. Secondly, the elaborate machinery of presidential elections, which was intended as a check on direct democracy, was meant to be a reality. Each state was to appoint electors and the choice of President was to be the result of the independent judgement of the Electoral College. This elaborate electoral machinery reminded Maine of the tradition of elective kingship in Europe, where a select body determined who might conceivably serve for life.

As the Founding Fathers were aware, monarchy did not necessitate the hereditary principle or life tenure. Dr Johnson's *English Dictionary* defined monarchy simply as government by a single person. Elective monarchy had a long history, with examples from Anglo-Saxon Britain, the Holy Roman Empire, Poland, and the Vatican. In Maine's opinion, the framers of the Constitution rejected Poland's disorderly model of elective monarchy but were guided by the Electoral College of the Holy Roman Empire. He observed that Hamilton and Madison had made a study of the Romano-German Empire in *Federalist* 19 and concluded that 'the American Republican Electors are the German Imperial Electors, except that they are chosen by the several States'.[73] Like Mill and Bagehot, Maine observed that the Electoral College had become 'a futile fiction', which had unhappy effects on presidential elections and a tendency to promote mediocre candidates. But he took wry pleasure in noting that the American system elected Washington, who was much less radical than the Emperor Joseph II.[74]

* * *

The Supreme Court was of interest to Maine because of its novelty, and he quoted with approval Tocqueville's observation that no other nation had constituted a judicial power like it. Yet he insisted that however novel the legal system established by the United States Constitution, it had its roots in the English past. The framers of the Constitution adopted the political doctrine of the separation of powers, but largely received their instruction in the principle from Montesquieu, who in *Esprit des Lois* cited England as the standard of political liberty. Maine detected the chief source of the American system of an independent judiciary in a line from Montesquieu, which Madison cited in *Federalist* 47: 'There is not liberty, if the judicial power be not separated from the Legislative and the Executive.' To Maine, it was impossible to read those words without recognizing that they were suggested to Montesquieu by the practice in England.[75]

Maine was well versed in Tocqueville and Mill, whose general approval of the American legal system largely dovetailed with his own. He believed that, given their colonial history, Americans must have been alive to the difficulties in discussing questions of constitutional law in legislative bodies. Yet he attributed many of the benefits of the justice system to a Supreme Court that in its method was essentially English. Like Mill, he admired the proposition that no law was declared in the abstract but rather on the facts of the case submitted for adjudication. 'The success of the Supreme Court of the United States', he argued, 'largely results from its following this mode of deciding questions of constitutionality and unconstitutionality. The process is slower, but it is freer from suspicion of pressure and much less provocative of jealousy, than the submission of broad and emergent political propositions to a judicial body.'[76] Maine did not comment on the Court's susceptibility to partisan bias, which Americans often noted.[77]

As with the Supreme Court, Maine saw the Congress as the offspring of the mother country, and he credited Montesquieu once again for bringing Americans around to British traditions. Unlike Bagehot, Maine thought the sharp separation of the legislature from the executive propitious. Furthermore, he was an ardent proponent of second chambers because they slowed down legislation. In his words, they were 'founded on a denial or a doubt of the proposition that the voice of the people is the voice of God.... They are the fruit of the agnosticism of the political understanding.'[78] Of all the second chambers in existence he believed the Senate was the most effective in stemming the tide of modern democracy and in decorum and authority had fully achieved the hopes of the founders. Unlike the presidency, the Senate had justified their aim of creating a chamber of distinguished men, who, with longer tenure and greater knowledge, would put a check on the prejudices of a restless, ill-informed electorate.[79]

Maine particularly admired the Senate because, like the House of Lords, it was not based on equality of representation. Article 1 of the Constitution provided that 'the Senate shall be composed of two senators from each state, chosen by the legislature thereof, for six years'. That little Rhode Island had the same number of senators as populous New York gave him pleasure, leading him to conclude that the Senate was based 'not on equality but inequality'. As a man who trumpeted liberty over equality, Maine applauded political institutions that were what he called 'a negation of equality'. And as an enemy of incautious legislation, he would have seconded Washington's much-quoted remark to Jefferson that 'we pour legislation into the senatorial saucer to cool it'.[80] Thus, to Maine, the Senate was a model that might influence a rethinking of the House of Lords, whose revival he thought essential to impede democracy in Britain.

Maine observed that while modern democracies resented inequalities of fortune, they were willing to tolerate historical inequalities. There were property qualifications for voting in most of the states when the Federal Constitution was framed. In an era of universal manhood suffrage, the hereditary privileges of the individual became more troubling, but the public were more forgiving of the undemocratic practices of historic institutions, especially those sanctioned by a revered Constitution. To Maine, the Senate of the United States reflected a great fact of American history: the political realities of the thirteen states at the birth of the republic. The survival of the institution in its eighteenth-century guise illustrated that 'nothing but an historical principle can be successfully opposed to the principle of making all public powers and all parliamentary assemblies the mere reflection of the average opinion of the multitude'.[81] It was a line of thought that gave him hope that the House of Lords and constitutional monarchy could be sustained in Britain.

The House of Representatives appealed to Maine rather less than the Senate, if only on the grounds that it was assumed to be the more democratic body. He insisted, however, that it was 'unquestionably a reproduction of the House of Commons'. As evidence he cited section 7 of Article 1 that laid down a British principle: 'All Bills raising Revenue shall originate in the House of Representatives; but the Senate may propose or concur with amendments as in other Bills.'[82] On the other hand, the House of Representatives was a more exclusively legislative body than either the Senate or the House of Commons. Unlike the Senate it had no rights over the province of the President and this restriction of power reminded Maine of the House of Commons at the time of the American Revolution.[83]

Maine wished to play down the democratic nature of the Congress and thus denied that the founders of the republic intended the House of Representatives to be a more democratic assembly than the House of Commons. He cited as evidence section 2 of Article 1, that it was to be composed of members chosen every second year by the people of the several states and that the electors in each state were to 'have the qualifications requisite for Electors of the most numerous branch of the State Legislature'.[84] As elsewhere, he called on the historical record, noting that *Federalist* 54, written by Madison, expressly said that the differences in the qualification to vote at the time were 'very material' and that in every state 'a certain proportion of the inhabitants are deprived of this right by the Constitution of the State'.[85]

Like many of the founders of the republic, who could not escape their colonial experience, Maine tended to translate King, Lord, and Commons into President, Senate, and House of Representatives. But by the 1880s, the translation was no longer apt, for Queen Victoria was not the executive but a figurehead. Like Paine, but from a radically different perspective, he used the American political tradition as a stick to beat the British. He paid particular attention to the differences between the United States government and the British government. Here the elaborate, but transparent, legislative procedures in Congress caught his eye. In America proposals that were likely to be successful derived from congressional committees, and went through the Congress before being sent to the President for approval or rejection. In Britain, where the House of Commons had taken under its control the entire executive government, it was difficult to determine where a legislative proposal started.

> An English Bill begins in petty rivulets or stagnant pools. Then it runs underground for most of its course, withdrawn from the eye by the secrecy of the Cabinet. Emerging into the House of Commons, it can no more escape from its embankments than the water of a canal; but once dismissed from that House, it overcomes all remaining obstacles with the rush of a cataract, and mixes with the trackless ocean of British institutions.[86]

What disturbed Maine about British legislative practice was that it applied not only to ordinary laws, but also to laws affecting the Constitution itself. 'Of all the infirmities of our Constitution in its decay, there is none more serious than the absence of any special precautions to be observed in passing laws which touch the very foundations of our political system.'[87] This was in striking contrast to America, where elaborate obstacles had to be overcome in amending the Constitution. He took as an example the recent English County Franchise Bill, of which he heartily disapproved. If such a Bill were introduced in America, the chances of its passing would have been far less likely, for it would have to be dealt with as a constitutional amendment. In practice, such a measure would require the concurring vote of fifty-eight legislative chambers, independently of a two-thirds majority in the House and Senate. In England, the English County Franchise Bill was driven through the Commons by the party whip with a bare plurality in a single House.[88]

Maine preferred checks to balances. Unlike Bagehot, who thought the hurdles imposed by the American Constitution clumsy and obstructive, he believed them essential securities against hasty innovation. In his opinion, the 'contrived securities' placed on the states by the Federal Constitution 'determined the whole course of American history'. He provided chapter and verse of the constitutional amendments since the foundation of the republic and concluded that the form of Federal institutions had always been preserved, despite the Civil War and remarkable social change. Returning to his watery metaphor he observed that the original constitutional provisions of America 'have acted on her like those dams and dykes which strike the eye of the traveller along the Rhine, controlling the course of a mighty river, which begins amid mountain torrents, and turning it into one of the most equable waterways in the world'. He could not resist a comparison with his own country, where the English Constitution 'like the great river of England, may perhaps seem to the observer to be now-a-days always more or less in flood, owing to the crumbling of the banks and the water poured into it from millions of drain pipes'.[89]

In his survey of the American Constitution, Maine noted provisions that he thought undervalued. Among them was the clause that prohibited the United States from granting titles of nobility, which may have caused him some uneasiness given his positive view of aristocracy. Few, he argued, would dismiss the importance of those portions of

Constitution that guaranteed every state a republican form of government or prevented states from entering into treaties or alliances. But he wished to draw attention to the importance of the provision that empowered the United States 'to promote the progress of science and the useful arts'; and the provision that gave the government the authority to grant patents, which had made Americans 'the first in the world' in inventions. Further, the prohibition against levying duties on commodities passing between states was 'the secret both of American Free-trade and of American Protection'.[90]

The provision that prohibited the power of the states to make laws impairing the obligation of contracts was, to Maine, one of the most important constitutional rules. Its principle had been extended by the Supreme Court in the case of *Dartmouth v. Woodward* (1819) and formed the basis of the credit of the great railway companies. Not one to miss an opportunity to deride democracy, Maine said the prohibition freed up the economy and was 'the bulwark of American individualism against democratic impatience and Socialistic fantasy'. He was confident that, as long as this prohibition lasted, 'communistic schemes of American origin, which are said to have become attractive to the English labouring classes because they are supposed to proceed from the bosom of a democratic community, have about as much prospect of obtaining practical realisation in the United States as the vision of Cloud-Cuckooborough to be built by the birds between earth and sky'.[91]

Maine had paid sufficient tribute to the American Constitution that he felt comfortable jeering at the odd provision. Like virtually every other British commentator—and many American ones—he saw the Electoral College as a miscarriage that had damaged the presidency. He was not, however, critical of the original conception of the college, but rather of its failure once the party system took hold, for which the framers of the Constitution had not prepared. In his view, a candidate elected by a properly working Electoral College may fall into error, but one nominated 'by the whole people, will, as a rule, be a man selected because he is not open to obvious criticism, and will therefore in all probability be a mediocrity'.[92] Still, he felt the mediocrities elected in the United States were an improvement on their counterparts on the European continent, particularly in France.

Though the Senate was his favoured branch of the American government, he could not acquit it of malfeasance. 'It would be affectation to claim for the American Federal Legislature as a whole that its hands are quite clean.' Too many Englishmen had done business in Washington who could attest to the fact that money was often misappropriated. Section 6 of Article 1 of the Constitution provided securities against corruption on the part of Senators and Representatives, but the system that prevailed produced 'a class of professional politicians, whose probity in some cases has proved unequal to the strain put upon it by the power of dealing with the public money'. It was a point that led Maine to make one of his few concessions to the governance of Britain, whose contemporary political culture, even in its decline, suffered less from corruption than the United States.[93]

Maine's writings on America were later than those of Mill and Bagehot, and had relatively little to say about the Civil War. He did not roundly condemn slavery, but there is no reason to suggest that he approved of it, despite his general dislike of expanding individual rights. But the one serious fault that Maine found with the framers of the Constitution turned on the issue of slavery, which they had thrust out of sight. They did not have the courage of their convictions and neither guaranteed, regulated, nor abolished slavery. When the Supreme Court decided seventy years later, in the Dred Scott case, whether the owner of slaves taking them into one of the territories retained the right of ownership, the Court did not have sufficient materials for a decision. In Maine's view, the result satisfied no one but the lawyers. 'It is extremely significant that, in the one instance in which the authors of the Constitution declined of set purpose to apply their political wisdom to a subject which they knew to be all-important, the result was the bloodiest and costliest war of modern times.'[94]

The message that Maine took away from American slavery was that in designing a democratic constitution no issue should be left unsettled. Only when public powers were carefully defined could democracy be made tolerable, or as he put it, 'made nearly as calm as water in a great artificial reservoir; but if there is a weak point anywhere in the structure, the might force which it controls will burst through and spread destruction far and near'.[95] It was a warning that he hoped Englishmen would heed in the aftermath of the legislation of 1884–5, which in opening the floodgates of democracy had unsettled the British Constitution without providing for an acknowledged authority to adjudicate the points of controversy.

In his peroration at the end of *Popular Government*, Maine returned to one of his central themes: that the American Constitution was a modified version of the British Constitution that existed during the early years of the reign of George III. Its great success owed much to the portion of the British institutions enshrined in it. But it was also attributable to the sagacity of the framers of the Constitution who amended British institutions to suit the conditions of the emancipated colonies. 'This sagacity stands out in every part of the *Federalist*, and it may be tracked in every page of subsequent American history.' He ended *Popular Government* with a provocative line that could only alienate many of his fellow countrymen. The history of the United States 'may well fill the Englishmen who now live *in faece Romuli* with wonder and awe'.[96]

* * *

What is to be made of Maine, a melancholy and remorseless scholar, who emerged from his ivory tower with a disputatious book that received plaudits and brickbats in equal measure? Conservatives have interpreted *Popular Government* as a book that systematized Burke into a coherent philosophy.[97] Today, they may look to Maine as a proponent of limited legislation, who, though far from a populist, assumed that the less Americans are governed the better it is for both the state and the individual. For progressives, now as in the past, *Popular Government* remains a negative, despairing work that is long on memorable phrases but short on broad political principles.[98] It has been said that Maine threw 'a cold douche over the sanguine assumptions of liberal democrats'.[99] His conservative opinions are still seen by them as reactionary, while his more ardent critics have seen him as intolerant, authoritarian, and dangerous.[100] Pessimists in power are prone to despotism.

One of the things that set Maine apart from his contemporaries was his extraordinary negativity. His distrust of the legislative state would have shocked many of his fellow conservatives. Like Hobbes, the foundation of his conservatism was fear, in what he saw as the stunning contrast between men's hopes and attainments. Like the traditionalist Burke, he abhorred a priori constitutions remote from history, but unlike Burke, he favoured a 'written' Constitution in America. Temperament is fate, and dejection led him to a different political sensibility than Bagehot, whose conservative instincts were relieved by a more buoyant, sunnier personality. Maine's sensitivity to history propelled his pessimism about the future of democracy, which only

America dispelled. From US history, he found the value of setting a historical principle to serve as a brake on pure democracy.[101] Still, as an American critic noted, Maine's faith in the judgement of history led him to the doubtful premise that the future must reproduce the past.[102] For a man quick to criticize others for a want of historical detail, his own generalizations were often based on inadequate evidence.[103]

Maine's *Popular Government* did not reach a mass American audience, but it disconcerted US citizens who read it, especially those whose views had been shaped by exceptionalist rhetoric and nationalist pride. What were they to make of his view that the Founding Fathers modelled the presidency on George III or that Americans only formed 'a nation because they once obeyed a king'?[104] The premise that democracy was friable and destructive also seemed untenable to them, for, despite the tempests of the United States, government by the people did not appear to be essentially fragile.[105] For all his carefully chosen historical examples, nostalgia for an aristocratic past may be said to have biased his judgement, which did not much credit human creativity or the impulse for liberty. Arguably, the framers of the American Constitution were an exception to the very historical determinism that underpinned his strident conservatism. Tellingly, both Marx and Maine turned to the historical process for guidance—the former predicted the inevitability of socialism, the latter its impossibility.[106]

For all his intellectual brilliance, perhaps because of it, Maine retreated into principle whenever faced with injustice. With his emotional reserve and narrow view of progress he could not be said to have been a man with much compassion for the poor and oppressed.[107] Maine was on the defensive in an era wedded to the idea of progress and growing more egalitarian. It took audacity in the 1880s to say that democracy led to the grave. Yet he showed undeniable prescience in predicting that political charlatans would prey on credulous voters, and for pointing to the potential for demagoguery and manipulation in an age beset by an ignorant, distracted electorate. In pointing to the difficulties in sustaining popular government and exposing the disparity between democratic theory and practice he was a prophet, albeit an uncomfortable one. Even his critics concede that a reason for rediscovering *Popular Government* is that many of its ideas have a startling topicality.[108]

5

James Bryce
Anglo-Saxon Democracy

> Whatever success it [the American Constitution] has attained must be in large measure ascribed to the political genius, ripened by long experience, of the Anglo-Saxon race.
>
> (James Bryce, 1888)

> Parties go on contending because their members have formed habits of joint action, and have contracted hatreds and prejudices, and also because the leaders find their advantage in using these habits and playing on these prejudices. The American parties now continue to exist, because they have existed. The mill has been constructed, and its machinery goes on turning, even when there is no grist to grind.
>
> (James Bryce, 1888)

'I like Mr Bryce', Queen Victoria remarked, 'he knows so much and is so modest.'[1] James Bryce, who accompanied the Queen to Florence in 1893, was the sort of man Her Majesty admired: intelligent without being ostentatious, well travelled but knowing his place. His Oxford friend, the jurist Albert Dicey, described him as 'the life of the party.... He stirs us all up, rushes about like a shepherd's dog, collects his friends, makes us meet, leads us into plans and adventures, and keeps everything going. His life will, I predict, be one of great and deserved success.'[2] And so it turned out, for his sociability and high spirits served him well as a scholar, jurist, Liberal Member of Parliament (1885–1907), cabinet minister, and one of the most popular British Ambassadors to the United States (1907–13). Back in England he was created Viscount Bryce of Dechmont in the County of Lanark.[3]

Bryce—a generation younger than Mill, Bagehot, and Maine—was an Ulster Scot, born in Belfast in 1838, the son of a schoolmaster. He attended Glasgow University before going up to Trinity College, Oxford, where he was showered with academic honours, including the Vinerian Scholarship in Law. Among his Oxford friends were the historians Goldwin Smith and E. A. Freeman, and the critics Matthew Arnold and Walter Pater. In the 1870s, he became friends with Bagehot, whom he described as 'perhaps the most original mind of his generation'.[4] His academic career had an uncanny resemblance to Maine's at Cambridge a generation earlier, but with very different outcomes, dictated by their contrasting politics and personalities. Bryce was elected a fellow of Oriel in 1862, but after a few years in a London law practice he returned to Oxford as Regius Professor of Civil Law. Just as Maine made his scholarly reputation with *Ancient Law*, Bryce made his with *The Holy Roman Empire* (1864), a romantic tribute to the Middle Ages that was a triumphant feat of learning for a man of 26. With the years, both men turned their attention to America, though Bryce's views and assumptions were decidedly more favourable to democracy.

Bryce was essentially a post-Civil War writer, commenting on an America that was rapidly gaining geopolitical and economic status. Unlike Mill, Bagehot, or Maine, he had first-hand experience of the United States, which he visited for the first time in 1870 with Dicey. It was love at first sight, for he was open to new experiences and found himself among an intellectual elite in the most advanced democracy on earth. He was soon at the centre of the web of relationships that developed between British and American liberals after the Civil War, which propelled his sense of transatlantic Anglo-Saxon unity.[5] Well connected, he had introductions to leading Americans of the day, including Emerson, Longfellow, and James Russell Lowell. Eleven years later he returned, with an invitation from Charles W. Eliot, the President of Harvard, to deliver a course of lectures. On this trip he covered new ground, visiting California and the South. A third visit followed in 1883, which included a 'picnic' in Montana to celebrate the completion of the Northern Pacific Railway that joined Chicago and Seattle. From there he travelled to Washington, Oregon, and Hawaii.

It was on his second visit, fifty years after Tocqueville travelled to America, that Bryce began to think about writing a major work on the United States, and on his third that he began to collect material.[6]

The result was the magisterial *The American Commonwealth*, published in three volumes in 1888, which he revised from time to time until his death in 1922. Bryce dedicated the book to Dicey and Thomas Erskine Holland, but most of his material came from friends in the United States. Few British writers were so energetic, or so well placed. He not only knew the topography but also had invaluable contacts across the country in the wake of his travels. 'I am a good listener...', he said to an American audience years later, 'I talked to everybody I could find in the United States, not only to statesmen in the halls of Congress, not only at dinner parties, but on the decks of steamers, in smoking cars, to drivers of wagons, upon the Western prairies, to ward politicians and city bosses.'[7] As one critic jested: 'his genius largely consisted in an infinite capacity for taking trains'.[8]

The list of friends and contacts acknowledged in the preface to *The American Commonwealth* reads like a *Who's Who* of the United States in the 1880s. It included Theodore Roosevelt, the justice Oliver Wendell Holmes, the Librarian of the State Department Theodore White, the diplomat John Jay, the President of the University of Michigan James B. Angell, and a host of college professors from across the country, all of whom provided assistance on specific issues.[9] Seth Low the former Mayor of Brooklyn and Frank Goodnow of Columbia University contributed chapters on municipal government. Woodrow Wilson wrote a chapter on women's suffrage in a later edition. The contracting out had an ulterior motive, for to obtain an American copyright Bryce needed a least one chapter authored by an American.[10]

When asked by Americans 'what do you think of our institutions?' the genial Bryce did not take it as a sign of insecurity or a need for praise as other European travellers had done in the past. Rather, he took it to mean that Americans assumed their democracy represented a wondrous experiment and that every one should study it because the promise of America was the promise of mankind. Like other British commentators who had supported the Union cause, he believed America 'the Land of the Future', which needed to be better understood in Europe. But unlike most of them, he was less frightened by the future, at least when he began his researches. He was an ardent democrat in an era when democracy was still thought to be seditious by conservatives.[11] His stated purpose in writing *The American Commonwealth* was to present a portrait of the United States and its government in the 1880s, both in theory and in practice. In so doing he concentrated on three things: the constitutional machinery, the methods by which it worked, and the forces that directed it.[12] In 1883, Bryce conducted a graduate seminar on Tocqueville at Johns Hopkins University. It was an opportunity to fashion a critique of *Democracy in America*, which, though he admired its lucidity and penetration, he subjected to rigorous scrutiny.[13] Like Burke and Bagehot, he distrusted speculative inquiry, which he believed unscientific; and in *The American Commonwealth* he avoided the Frenchman's lofty deductions in favour of a ruthless empiricism that presented 'the facts of the case'.[14] His successive visits to America had made him sensitive to the changing nature of his subject and consequently cautious in making generalizations that had to be cast overboard on his return. 'I can honestly, say', he remarked at the beginning of *The American Commonwealth*, no doubt with Tocqueville in mind, 'that I shall be far better pleased if readers of a philosophic turn find in the book matter on which they feel they can safely build theories for themselves, than if they take from it theories ready made'.[15]

Although Bryce was a historian, he did not favour the explicit historical method that had animated Maine. In a letter to a friend in 1887, he dismissed Maine's *Popular Government* as a poor thing in everything 'but its style.... He does not seem to me to come near understanding America: he does not even quite understand the U.S. Constitution; and his charges against democracy are generally as self-contradictory as his historical instances are one-sided and flimsy.'[16] Yet the Tory Maine, though never mentioned in the text of *The American Commonwealth*, lurks in the background rather more than meets the eye. Despite their differing methods and political views—Bryce was a Gladstonian Liberal—their opinions on America often corresponded, not least on the evils of the party system and nature of the US Constitution, which both men saw as British in character and an instrument of conservatism.

In what may be seen as a rebuke to Maine, Bryce thought it fruitless to apply the lessons of America to British politics, even though, as he noted, there were lessons of encouragement and warning on offer. On this point he was explicit: 'no fact has been either stated or suppressed, and no opinion put forward, with the purpose of serving any English party-doctrine or party-policy, or in any furnishing arguments for use in any English controversy'.[17] His study was meant to be an objective record useful to students of government, not a treatise for or against

British democracy. While Europe might well follow American precedents, he was not of the opinion that direct inferences from the United States could be applied beyond American shores, if only because social conditions were so different. One reason for writing history was to rescue mankind from misguided historical analogies.[18]

But while Bryce disliked reasoning from parallel cases, he thought the traditions of transatlantic unity worth preserving. He was far from singular in speaking positively about Anglo-American accord in the late nineteenth century, but he probably did as much to promote it as anyone else. Relations between the two nations had deteriorated during the Civil War and after it there was a vague sense in Britain that an ever more powerful United States threatened the Empire. Bryce served as a powerful link in the Anglo-Saxon liberalism that improved relations between the two greatest English-speaking nations in the late nineteenth century.[19] The signal achievement of *The American Commonwealth*, as a leading authority remarks, was to encourage 'a realignment of understanding, a new perception of the United States as ally and friend, whose growing influence could only add to and in no substantial way diminish those traditions'.[20]

No other book by a British writer on American government in the nineteenth century received so much attention, almost all of it positive. (In America alone, it sold over 212,000 copies by 1910.[21]) Theodore Roosevelt preferred it to Tocqueville. Gladstone, who read it with his customary seriousness, thought its publication an important event in Anglo-American relations.[22] Frederick Harrison wrote a notable review in the *Nineteenth Century*, republished in America, in which he put Bryce in the same league with Tocqueville and Mill. In further praise, he compared his fellow Oxonian's study of nineteenth-century America with Montesquieu's study of eighteenth-century England. Bryce's special strength, he argued, was in combining analysis of institutions with practical observation of social habits on the spot. *The American Commonwealth* did not, according to Harrison, go into the ultimate problems of government as deeply as Tocqueville, but Bryce was the rare example of a constitutional jurist, whose detailed study of the branches of government, machine politics, lobbying, spoils, bosses, and a host of other issues 'is precisely what we want to know'.[23]

If Bryce's American writing had little of the fireworks of Bagehot or Maine, there was none of their distain.[24] In a discussion of *The American Commonwealth* in the *English Historical Review*, Lord Acton remarked that 'the distinctive import of the book is its power of impressing American readers'.[25] Clearly, Bryce pleased many Americans by his generous exposition of their social institutions and constitutional arrangements, which included over 240 pages on state governments, a subject largely ignored by other commentators. His chapter on women's rights flattered women, while professors found much to admire in his comments on US higher education. Reviewers used the words, 'kind', 'fair', and 'unpatronising', which they had rarely used for British writers in the past. Happily for Bryce, the familiar complaints about supercilious foreigners had somewhat dissipated by the 1880s. One American commentator observed, in what was high praise indeed, that Bryce knew the United States so thoroughly that he might 'have been born among us'.[26]

Most reviewers, whether American or British, compared *The American Commonwealth* to *Democracy in America*, published a half-century earlier.[27] Bryce wished to achieve something less ambivalent about the social consequences of democracy for a different generation in a country much changed since Tocqueville's visit in the 1830s.[28] Woodrow Wilson, who reviewed the book in the *Political Science Quarterly*, noted the contrast with *Democracy in America*, which served to illustrate Bryce's significance as a careful student of a country that was very different from the 'crude and impatient democracy of Andrew Jackson's time'.[29] Another American critic saw their respective books as companionable. 'De Tocqueville wrote as a prophet, Bryce writes as a historian; De Tocqueville philosophizes, Bryce describes.... De Tocqueville is, in short, a Frenchman and a brilliant thinker, Bryce is an Englishman and a cautious student.'[30] If Tocqueville profited from a speculative turn, Bryce suffered from scholarly overkill. (*The American Commonwealth* runs to over 1,500 pages.) A reviewer in the *New England and Yale Review* found Bryce the more accurate and exhaustive writer but unlikely to be the last word, while Tocqueville was the more stylish and probing and therefore 'imperishable'.[31]

* * *

If Tocqueville was an impressionist, Bryce was a photographer.[32] He opened his study with a snapshot of the origins of American government. It resembled the glowing images drawn of the Founding Fathers at the Constitutional Convention in Philadelphia. While the

Constitution was open to criticism for its arrangements and omissions, not least in tolerating slavery as an institution, Bryce took a much more positive view of the document than Bagehot, who is cited only once in *The American Commonwealth*: 'After all the deductions, it ranks above every other written constitution for the intrinsic excellence of its scheme, its adaptation to the circumstances of the people, the simplicity, brevity and the precision of its language, its judicious mixture of definiteness in principle with elasticity in details.'[33] Bryce abhorred slavery, and the fact that it had been abolished by the time he wrote on America set him apart from British writers in the ante-bellum years. His favourable interpretation of the US Constitution should be seen against the background of the Amendments of the 1860s, which were in keeping with his progressive views.

Bryce was a man in search of a companionable Anglo-American democracy rooted in history and a common culture. In the process he made an impressive contribution to the debate over the foundations of democracy. Unlike the many earlier American commentators who interpreted the Constitution as a break from history, a supreme example of political discontinuity, Bryce saw its origins deep in the English past, which, like many of his contemporaries, he casually elided with the British past. 'There is little in that constitution that is absolutely new', he declared, 'there is much that is as old as Magna Charta.'[34] Betraying a lawyerly conservatism, he believed the American Constitution demonstrated that everything that had the power to win the obedience and respect of the public drew on precedent, and the slower a system of government developed the more enduring it was likely to become.[35] Such views found a ready audience among American Anglophiles, who looked to Britain for solace and inspiration. When the historian Edward Eggleston published his account of early America in 1896, a book dedicated to Bryce, he remarked that he was telling 'the story of English achievement'.[36]

Bryce thought that Tocqueville had underestimated the English influences on US institutions.[37] Unlike the Frenchman, he gave greater emphasis to the colonial background of the Founding Fathers, who had been educated under the common law and the English Constitution. 'No men were less revolutionary in spirit than the heroes of the American Revolution. They made a revolution in the name of Magna Charta and the Bill of Rights.'[38] He believed they did not fully understand colonial administration because they had come under the influence of William Blackstone, whose constitutional theory was years behind its practice, not least in regard to the powers of the King. But in points of fundamental importance they appreciated and turned to advantage the spirit and methods of the 'venerable' mother country. In Bryce's opinion, the Founding Fathers had neither the rashness nor the capacity for constructing a Constitution a priori. Thus they created the Presidency on the model of the State Governor and the British Crown, while they created the Congress on the model of the houses of their state legislatures and the British Parliament.[39]

Bryce, like Maine, believed that the Founding Fathers had received their instruction in the critical principle of the separation of powers from Montesquieu, who cited England as its standard bearer.[40] Like most Victorian writers on American government, Bryce was unsympathetic to French revolutionary principles and wary of France generally as Britain's historic enemy. He admired the Anglophile Montesquieu but dismissed any notion that continental thinkers, in particular Rousseau, influenced America regarding abstract theories of human rights. Such rights came not from France, he insisted, but from the Declaration of Independence and the original constitutions of the states. It was the working of the colonial administration and the state governments following the Revolution that gave Americans the practical knowledge of how to define and limit the powers of government.[41]

From all this, Bryce concluded that the Founding Fathers owed their success at the Constitutional Convention 'to the political genius, ripened by long experience, of the Anglo-American race'.[42] This theme of an Anglo-Saxon fraternity, which earlier British writers on the American Constitution had frequently endorsed, though more tentatively before the abolition of slavery, was to come into sharper focus in *The American Commonwealth*. A desire to link the ancient institutions of England and those current in the United States prompted Bryce's original research into local and county government. Thus he traced the New England town meeting, celebrated by Tocqueville and Mill, to the English vestry meeting, the Southern county to the English shire, and the Northern township to the English parish. Like everything else in America, he observed, they were English institutions that had 'suffered a sea change'.[43]

Bryce's Anglo-Saxon interpretation of the American Constitution reflected a trend in transatlantic relations in the late nineteenth century, which several of his friends, including Dicey and Arnold, had promoted.

After a tour of the United States in the late 1860s, Charles Dilke, the Liberal Member of Parliament, captured the growing mood: 'In America, the peoples of the world are being fused together, but they are run into an English mould.... America offers the English race the moral directorship of the globe, by ruling mankind through Saxon institutions and the English tongue. Through America England is speaking to the world.'[44] In an article 'Kin Beyond the Sea' (1878), Gladstone, eager to mollify the United States after the diplomatic tensions of the post-Civil War years, called for 'a new moral unity of the English-speaking people' and famously described the American Constitution as 'the most wonderful work ever struck off by the brain and purpose of man'.[45]

After the Civil War, arbitration eased tensions between the two nations, and the two countries drew closer together politically. With the old resentments diminished, subservience to British opinion was fading in the United States by the 1880s. From time to time there were serious issues that divided the two nations, as over Venezuela.[46] But in an era of growing international rivalries, American and British diplomats saw advantage in closer relations, which complemented economic and cultural links. Sir Edward Grey, the British Foreign Minister, later spoke of an 'Anglo-Saxon feeling' that had its basis in language and a kindred point of view, in which the majority on both sides of the Atlantic 'has a hatred of what is not just and free'.[47]

In the 1880s, many Britons, including Bryce and Dilke, continued to see Americans as transatlantic relations, or, as Arnold put it, 'the English on the other side of the Atlantic'.[48] The appeal to Anglo-American kinship served a particular purpose in an era of growing Irish consciousness.[49] It became more controversial with E. A. Freeman, who adopted, at least New Englanders, as his 'kith and kin' during a speaking tour of the United States in 1881. 'We are English in Britain, you are English in America.' But he rather spoilt the effect with a wild remark that alienated even his friends: 'This would be a grand land if only every Irishman would kill a Negro, and be hanged for it.'[50] Bryce, who strongly disapproved of the arrogance of the British abroad, was among those who found the remark distasteful.

* * *

Bryce found two main principles underlying American politics: the sovereignty of the people and a distrust of government. The system safeguarded the individual from aggression by making each organ of government a jealous observer of the others. Bryce was a Scottish Presbyterian, and he admired the 'hearty Puritanism' in the US Constitution, with its checks and balances and its suspicious view of human nature. For all his defence of democracy, he did not believe that mankind had shown any moral improvement under it.[51] He quoted the wit who said the American government was based on the theology of Calvin and the philosophy of Hobbes. 'It is the work of men who believed in original sin, and were resolved to leave open for transgressors no door which they could possible shut.' He compared this spirit with the French enthusiasm of 1789, and found the difference in racial temperament and fundamental ideas. For Bryce, the Founding Fathers were Whigs not Jacobins, and 'the spirit of 1787 was an English spirit, and therefore a conservative spirit, tinged, no doubt, by the hatred of tyranny developed in the revolutionary struggle'.[52]

Bryce thought the aim of the American Constitution was less to do with attaining great common ends and more to do with averting the evils that flowed from any government strong enough to threaten the individual citizen. All constitutions were faulty, he believed, with the defects of their better qualities. As Bagehot had pointed out with obvious dismay, the American example favoured security and equilibrium over executive speed and concentration of power. Bryce was more sanguine: 'the waste of power by friction, the want of unity and vigour in the conduct of affairs by executive and legislature, are the price which the Americans pay for the autonomy of their States, and for the permanence of the equilibrium among the various branches of their government'. If George Washington were to return, Bryce thought he would recognize his handiwork, for after a century of American governance, neither the executive nor the legislature threatened the liberties of the people. Unlike many a European state, the American Constitution 'has stood and stands unshaken'.[53]

Bryce concluded his chapter 'On the Frame of National Government' with an observation that would have pleased the patriotic American jurists and historians of the republic. Not the least of the merits of the US Constitution, he noted, was that it had made itself 'beloved'. Improvements could remove some of its inconveniences, 'but reverence for the Constitution has become so potent a conservative influence, that no proposal of fundamental change seems likely to be entertained'. And, he added, 'this reverence is itself one of the most wholesome and hopeful elements in the character of the American people'.[54] By the end of the nineteenth century it was becoming common for British Liberals and Tories alike to applaud the conservative elements in the American Constitution, for fear of something worse, what Bagehot had called 'mob rule'. It reinforced their desire to find affinities between the American Constitution and the mother country that dated to the colonial period and beyond.

To Bryce, the affinities started with the executive. Like Maine, he viewed the President as an elected, republican monarch. As he put it, the statesmen of the Constitutional Convention looked to existing models and produced a 'reduced and improved copy of the English king. He is George III, shorn of a part of his prerogative by the intervention of the Senate in treaties and appointments, of another part by the restriction of his action to Federal affairs, while his dignity as well as his influence are diminished by his holding office for four years instead of for life.'[55] Like Maine, Bryce thought the method of electing the President reminiscent of that used to elect the German Emperor, although the President differed in having a salary too small to maintain a court or to corrupt the legislature.

To Bryce, the framers of the Constitution wished the President to be a personage above and outside party, who, selected by impartial electors, would represent the nation as a whole. He regretted that only George Washington realized the ideal before the party system began to take hold. Later Presidents were elected as a party leader by a party vote, which led them to submit to the policies of those who put them in power. Thus, instead of getting an Olympian President raised above faction, America reproduced the English system of executive government by a party majority, but without the level of leadership. Bryce admitted the disadvantages of the American plan, but, rather against the grain of his remarks elsewhere about spoils and party corruption, argued that the great responsibility of the President and the sense that he represented the entire nation tended to restrain abuse.[56]

While there were marked similarities between Britain and America in regard to the growth of parties, the differences were also notable. In England, the titular head of state stood outside party politics in what Bryce called 'isolated dignity'.[57] Combining the executive and the ceremonial head of state in the American presidency was, in fact, a concession to a traditional form of kingship, which is what the Founders assumed to have existed in the reign of George III. Though he did not develop his reservations about this arrangement, Bryce detected a potential problem in combining the two roles, for the Constitution encouraged Americans to revere the President as head of state even when they disapproved of him as the executive. As an American authority observed in the 1890s: 'The attempt to compass these two functions is a killing task, fraught with great perils to the individual incumbent and to the public welfare.'[58] Later European republics, those of France, Germany, and Italy for example, separated these roles as a safeguard against the abuse of power.

Bryce provided his readers with a detailed list of the powers of the presidency, from those of Commander in Chief and the making of treaties to granting pardons and the appointment of officials. Throughout *The American Commonwealth*, he was determined to give a balanced picture of these powers, comparing them to those of Britain's Prime Minister and its constitutional monarch. In emergencies these powers increased while in quieter times they diminished. Lincoln, in his view, 'wielded more authority than any single Englishman has done since Oliver Cromwell'.[59] Like Bagehot, Bryce tended to see Lincoln as a benevolent despot, and in *The American Commonwealth* compared him to a temporary Roman dictator. 'Fortunately', as he put it, 'the habits of legality' were deeper in America than in the later Roman Empire and the ship of state righted itself.[60]

Like every other British commentator, Bryce thought individual presidents generally disappointing, rarely above average in character or abilities. Why, he asked, were great men not elected presidents? His analysis was a reprise of Bagehot, though with more detail and less disillusionment. The dismal list of presidents was especially curious in a nation in which a 'career open to talents' was greater than elsewhere and in which ambition was widespread. Still, America was an expanding country that provided lucrative alternatives to politics. Unlike England, politics was not a 'great social game'.[61] Since the heroes of the revolution died out with Adams, Jefferson, and Madison, only Lincoln had striking talents and only Grant would have been remembered had he not been President. 'Who now knows or cares to know anything about the personality of James K. Polk or Franklin Pierce? The only thing remarkable about them is that being so commonplace they should have climbed so high.' Even Jackson, in Bryce's estimation, though an able politician and soldier, was 'a narrow and uncultivated intellect'.[62] With rare exceptions, American presidents were 'intellectual pigmies'.[63]

In keeping with Bagehot, Bryce thought the disconnection between the executive and the Congress, which prevented true leadership, was at the heart of the problem.[64] Eloquence, knowledge, and profundity of thought were not usually required of a President, who did not have to defend his policies in Congress, unlike a Prime Minister in Parliament. The American system valued common sense, honesty, and administrative skill. Most of a President's work was of the kind that devolved upon a railway manager or a chairman of a commercial company. Consequently, potential candidates had second thoughts about standing for office, especially as they could make more money in commerce. Bryce agreed with Mill that great men were rare in politics; in quiet times they were not needed in the United States. He concluded that 'the ordinary American voter does not object to mediocrity'.[65]

In Bryce's opinion, the 'natural selection' of parliamentary government tended to bring men of greater gifts to office than the 'artificial selection' of the United States. The American party system, which had perfected party loyalty and organization, created the 'artificial selection'. It promoted mediocrity while discouraging men of talent from running for office. 'To a party it is more important that its nominee should be a good candidate than that he should turn out a good President. A nearer danger is a greater danger.' It was a disaster to the party if the candidate elected turned out to be a failed President, but it was a greater disaster to the party should it lose an election and be deprived of the opportunity for national patronage.[66] When a talented President unexpectedly emerged, as in the case of Lincoln, it was largely down to chance.

The problems of administration flowed largely from a party system in which aspirants for the presidency sought to avoid making enemies while pleasing the party faithful. A further defect was the frequency of elections. They not only threw the country into a state of turmoil, but also produced artificial issues that had not previously existed. With a combination of religious zeal and military efficiency, professional politicians, who had a personal stake in offices to be divided, created a fractious campaign that wasted money without educating the public. To Bryce, party spirit was less threatening in Britain because the voters were more politically informed. It was unfortunate that the American Constitution required elections with such regularity, for they produced discontinuities of policy, which the practice of rewarding supporters and removing opponents from office exacerbated.[67]

Like Bagehot, and perhaps under his influence, Bryce took exception to a system that allowed the President to remove officials and appoint his own supporters. He noted that the word 'removals' did not appear in the Constitution. 'Spoils', to which Bryce devoted a critical chapter, illustrated the dangers of leaving innumerable offices at the pleasure of a partisan President to use for party purposes. It made place-hunting into a career, created a crop of party hacks and bosses, and turned the President into a 'wire puller', a term used by Maine in his critique of American party democracy. To Bryce, wire pulling and place filling were unworthy of a talented executive, who was meant to spend his time on national issues. He cited the story in which Lincoln was asked by a friend: 'You look anxious, Mr President; is there bad news from the front?' 'No,' answered Lincoln, 'it isn't the war; it's that post-mastership at Brownsville, Ohio.'[68]

* * *

Bryce discussed the American Congress against the background of the House of Lords and the House of Commons. Like other British commentators, he had an affection for the Senate—'this masterpiece of the Constitution-makers'—which he believed had attained its principal objectives, not least of which was to guard against gusts of democratic passion.[69] To Bryce, Senators were the nearest approach to an official American aristocracy. For all their pretensions, intrigues, and misdemeanours, they provided a centre of gravity that checked the 'democratic recklessness' of the House, and the 'Monarchical ambition' of the President. Unlike the House of Representatives, whose members had only a term of two years, Senators were a greater bulwark against agitation 'because experience has taught them how fleeting a thing popular sentiment is, and how useful a thing continuity in policy is'.[70] Such views suggested that there was more of Maine's *Popular Government* in *The American Commonwealth* than Bryce would admit.

Bryce took the view that the Senate's original function in securing the rights of the smaller states was no longer important because the extent of states' rights had been settled. In an era when there were only thirty-eight states, he did not anticipate the potential of a handful of senators from states with modest populations blocking the will of the majority. (Today the twenty least populous states with forty senators have just 10 per cent of the nation's population.[71]) In the 1880s, the

Senate was proud of conducting its business without closing off or limiting debates. When every man knew his colleagues intimately, he had a strong sense of maintaining the manners and moral authority of the Chamber and was slow to resort to extreme methods that might lower it in public esteem. As Bryce noted: 'Till recently, systematic obstruction, or, as it is called in America, "filibustering"... was almost unknown.'[72] Today, a Senate Rule—which does not appear in the Constitution—requires sixty senators to stop unlimited filibustering.[73]

Bryce cited with approval Woodrow Wilson's recently published book *Congressional Government*, which did not romanticize the Senate but saw it as a product of a party system. Both men agreed that the Senate drew on the best 'available' talent in the nation and established an intellectual supremacy. As Bryce put it, it was not an 'Olympian dwelling-place of statesmen' but 'a company of shrewd and vigorous men who have fought their way to the front by the ordinary methods of American politics, and on many of whom the battle has left its stains'.[74] It was not comparable to the House of Lords in regard to ability because the Lords had so many members who did not take an active part in deliberations, but setting it beside the House of Commons, the average capacity of its seventy-six members was below the standard of the seventy-six best men in the Commons, who had a greater breadth of education and culture.[75]

Bryce was less favourably disposed to the House of Representatives, which he saw as the political instrument of the common man. An Englishman, he noted, might expect the House to resemble the House of Commons. Its rules and procedures, after all, drew heavily on English precedents. While Bryce saw similarities, he emphasized the differences, for the life and spirit of the two assemblies were very different. For a start the room in which the House met in the south wing of the Capitol was over three times as large as the House of Commons. Disorder was endemic. On entering 'your first impression is of noise and turmoil, a noise like that of short sharp waves in a Highland loch, fretting under a squall against a rocky shore.... I have never heard American voices sound so harsh or disagreeable as they do here.' Speeches were not oratory but a series of declamations; debates were languid and unprofitable. Most of the practical work was done in the standing committees, while the House spent its time in 'pointless discussions'.[76]

Americans, particularly his New England friends, had told Bryce that members of the House of Representatives were inferior to members of the House of Commons. Perhaps he had read Mark Twain's lampoons of American politicians or the indictment of congressmen in the anonymously published novel *Democracy* (1880) by Henry Adams. In any case, he was rather taken by surprise when visiting Congress to find a degree of 'character, shrewdness and keen though limited intelligence among the representatives'. But great men, who adorned the House of Commons, were absent. Congressman made their way by energy not intellect. In Europe men of all sorts, from nobles and landowners to men of learning and science, turned up in legislatures; in America representatives conformed to a type, scarcely above the class of second-rate lawyers, farmers, or merchants. And despite Americans coming from nationalities across the globe, Bryce found that the House of Representatives reflected a population more uniform than in most of the great European states.[77]

Unlike the House of Commons, the House of Representatives had only a legislative function. Its strangest feature to an Englishman, according to Bryce, was that it had parties, 'but they are headless'. Americans assumed that the legislature ought to be distinct from the executive, but 'there is neither Government nor Opposition; neither leaders nor whips. No minister, no person holding any Federal office or receiving any Federal salary, can be a member of it.'[78] The majority had a chief, the Speaker of the House, but as he rarely joined in debate, the chairman of the important Ways and Means Committee came nearer to being the leader of the House. If it were the legislatures of France or Germany, which were divided into disparate sections of opinion, it would not work; but in America there were usually only two parties of nearly equal strength and upon all large issues they could be expected to vote as a block.

When Bryce looked at the House of Representatives, with its air of confusion and unremarkable members, he had to subdue his own doubts about American democracy. His gravest worry about the republic was the lack of leadership and the want of great men in office. In a revealing passage in *The American Commonwealth*, he recalled attending the House of Representatives 'with its huge gray hall, filled with perpetual clamour' and an irreverent public watching from the galleries. He wondered what was to become of the English-speaking people in a troublesome world that needed American guidance: 'If the men are not great, the interests and the issues are vast and fateful. Here, as so often in America, one thinks rather of the future than of the present.

Of what tremendous struggles may not this hall become the theatre in ages yet far distant, when the parliaments of Europe have shrunk to insignificance.'[79]

* * *

The chapter in *The American Commonwealth* on the party system, which Wilson called the book's 'crowning achievement', was a triumph of exposition.[80] Entrenched and embittered parties, which picked candidates to run for office, exacerbated Bryce's doubts about the future. In discussing the failings of democratic reform, Tocqueville and Mill had neglected the effects of the party organization in favour of studying social forces and public opinion. But by the 1880s, the role of parties in undermining the intentions of the Founding Fathers was arousing greater attention. Late Victorian British liberals, including Bryce, Dicey and Goldwin Smith, were increasingly disturbed by the partisanship unleashed by political parties on both sides of the Atlantic. Goldwin Smith, for one, insisted that the permanent party system constituted little more than a 'bisection of human nature' that left politics in a straightjacket.[81]

Encouraged by his contacts among progressives in the United States, Bryce was, along with Maine, among the leading constitutional authorities to give serious attention to the pitfalls of American parties and electioneering. A large part of *The American Commonwealth* was taken up with party practices, and it was more original than the many pages given over to the Congress, the courts, or the relationship between the three branches of government, which other writers had dissected in the past. After a brief history of the political parties, in which Bryce displayed the typical British reverence for Hamilton, he turned to the parties of the 1880s. His analysis was bleak. 'Nothing in recent history', he asserted, 'suggests that the statesmen who claim to be party leaders, or the politicians who act as party managers, are disposed either to loosen the grip with which their organization has clasped the country, or to improve the methods it employs.... The Machine will not be reformed from within: it must be assailed from without.'[82]

In Bryce's opinion, American parties, unlike European parties, counted for more than government. They were the great moving forces, and the fainter their principles the more perfect their organization: 'The less of nature the more of art; the less spontaneity the more mechanism.'[83] When perplexed Europeans asked Americans what principles separated the Republicans and Democrats, they never received an answer according to Bryce. This was because neither party had any principles. Instead, they had traditions and tendencies, battle cries and organizations. Their chief interest was in acquiring government patronage. 'Tenets and policies, points of political doctrine and points of political practice, have all but vanished. They have not been thrown away but have been stripped away by time and the progress of events, fulfilling some policies, blotting out others. All has been lost, except office or the hope of it.' American parties continued to exist in a corrupt and fetid state because they have existed and because they were implied by the system of government. 'The mill has been constructed, and its machinery goes on turning even when there is not grist to grind.'[84]

For Bryce, American democracy suffered hugely from the party machines and the bosses and armies of office seekers that they produced, people who had no direct responsibility for government administration. British visitors had long seen the frequency of American elections as a wasteful distraction.[85] Mill, among others, had complained about the nation's incessant electioneering. For Bryce, the number of elective offices at stake was a chief cause of government corruption, for it propelled the unruly politics manipulated by party bosses. And while he hesitated to make recommendations for reform, it was easy to deduce from his remarks that the answers lay in reducing the number of elections and offices, abandoning the principle of rotation in office, and making office dependent on merit, not political service or party affiliation.

Bryce was justly proud of the mass of information that he was able to gather from well-connected friends and their contacts about the working of party politics, not least at the ward and city levels. His views reflected those of educated American reformers, who were appalled by machine politics, which they often associated with newly arrived immigrant stock, most notably the Irish.[86] The portrait he painted of jobbery, bribery, misuse of public funds, and party patronage was, as he put it, 'not a bright picture'. But he concluded, with his customary balance and bedside manner, that neither was it 'so dark as that which most Europeans have drawn'. He noted that the standards of government in a republic were set higher than in a European monarchy, but that conditions were unfavourable to the expression of civic virtue in a new country with so many ambitious people without social position. Politicians everywhere fell into snares; and that while political institutions in the United States fell below the level of purity in England, 'her federal and state administration, in spite of the evils flowing from an uncertain tenure, is not... markedly inferior to the administrations of most European countries'.[87]

One of the chief failings Bryce found in the American party system turned on the selection of candidates. The motto was safety first. The safe candidate—typically someone without a record of achievement—would not receive so many votes from the centre, but he would not lose so many from the party base; and in the heat of the election, party loyalty could be counted upon. In presidential elections, state and sectional interests trumped personal merit. Better to have an inferior candidate from New York or Ohio than a superior candidate from Rhode Island or New Hampshire. Moreover, in the selection, it was more important to gratify a doubtful state than one that could be counted upon. Bryce assumed that Roman Catholics and atheists could not be elected. On the other hand, distinguished military men who had fought in the Northern army were desirable candidates—witness Grant—but one who had fought on the side of the Confederacy was unlikely to gain favour in the Northern states.[88]

In his analysis of campaigns and electioneering, Bryce was not telling American readers much they did not already know about the nature of their political life. 'There is no intelligent centre in America where the evils of our system are not understood', remarked one reviewer.[89] But as Bryce recognized, Americans had become complacent, generally willing to put up with the electoral corruption and lacklustre candidates. After all, the United States had become a great country despite its placemen, bosses, and ineffectual leadership. The reverence for the Constitution overcame the public's doubts about its application, buoyed by the growing prosperity and power of the United States. But as a leading American authority observed, the politicization of the Civil War had unhappy effects. Over the years, 'misguided memories' and 'partial amnesia' replaced principles and beliefs in the main political parties.[90] Selective memory and American optimism forgave the failings of politics.

Bryce was himself decidedly forgiving of American democracy, and, like many Americans, willing to set aside the worries of the present in favour of hopes for the future. While others found fault with a system of government that plunged the United States into a whirlpool of misguided frenzy every two years, he took a positive American view of the predicament. As one reviewer remarked, he was never more empathetic than when propounding unpleasant truths, which were often supported by an impressive body of evidence.[91] In his exposure of electoral malpractices, for example, Bryce noted that of the 1,007 primaries and conventions held in New York City preparatory to the election of 1884, 633 took place in saloons.[92]

For all his detailed criticism of electoral corruption and party chicanery, Bryce was determined to find light at the end of American democracy; and he was quick to draw attention to the many virtues that made the United States a luminous example to the rest of the world. An American reviewer of *The American Commonwealth* advertised them as follows:

The perpetual stir of politics, the growth of intelligent criticism among the common people, their interest in all parts of the Government, their essential right-mindedness growing out of their long habits of self-government, the slowness of the nation to mingle in external quarrels for the advantage of classes and individuals, or on points of diplomatic etiquette, the tremendous energy and endurance of the nation when the occasion is sufficient to kindle it, the paramount control by the whole people of all large interests. The people make themselves felt when they wish.[93]

As this reviewer suggested, Bryce was not simply a student of the Constitution and political institutions, but, like Tocqueville, a student of American society, which he admired for the spread of social equality. Like other Victorian writers he moved effortlessly from a discussion of democracy as a set of political arrangements to democracy as a social condition, and it is not obvious that the former had much to do with the latter.

According to Bryce, when the people made their wishes known, elected officials listened. In his view, public opinion mattered more in America, where there was little distinction of social class, than in Europe. 'Towering over presidents and State governors, over Congress and State legislatures, over conventions and the vast machinery of party, public opinion stands out, in the United States, as the great source of power, the master of servants who tremble before it.'[94] In the incessant din of voices, civic associations supporting every conceivable cause stood out in shaping opinion, a point that Tocqueville had made decades earlier. So too did newspapers, monthly magazines, and religious weeklies with their often partisan views.[95] But if public opinion was as powerful as he believed, it propelled, or at least tolerated, the persistence of the debased party system that he described elsewhere. Bryce might have resolved the problem by saying that Americans were too ignorant and distracted to have open and honest government, but it would have been counter to his belief in their enlightened character.[96] Bryce elided his extensive discussion of public opinion with reference to 'national character'. Indeed, national character is the key to understanding his analysis, not 'equality of condition' as in Tocqueville.[97] These were among the words that he used to define the US citizenry: kindness, humour, hopeful, religious, commercial, associative, unsettled, and changeful. 'After this', he added, 'it may seem a paradox to add that the Americans are a conservative people. Yet any one who observes the power of habit among them, the tenacity with which old institutions and usages, legal and theological formulas, have been clung to, will admit the fact.' In keeping with his theme of Anglo-Saxon unity, he linked American conservatism to the mother country: 'a love for what is old and established is in their English blood'.[98]

The characteristics that Bryce discovered in the American people were unlikely to produce a tyranny of the majority, and he used his discussion of national character as background to his comments about Tocqueville's overriding fear about democracy. To Bryce, a majority was tyrannical when it made wanton and improper use of its powers without reference to minority opinion. Since Tocqueville's day, European conservatives had come to expect democracies to have this characteristic sin. Bryce wished to disabuse them. In the 1830s, Mill found little evidence to support Tocqueville's vision, and fifty years later Bryce felt the same, though he conceded that social persecution might exist in 'a few dark corners' such as the smaller towns of the West. He suspected that Tocqueville 'attributed too much of the submissiveness which he observed to the active coercion of the majority, and too little to that tendency of the minority to acquiescence'.[99]

Bryce was intent on making America safe for democracy, and this propelled his criticism of Tocqueville, who he believed had a vision of democracy that was fixed and unchanging. When Tocqueville visited America the democratic spirit was in its infancy. The generation of the Founding Fathers, men of education and culture, had left the scene, replaced by ignorant men of low social standing. Echoing Bagehot's contempt for mob rule, Bryce believed the Jacksonian masses had become so persuaded of their superiority that they would listen to nothing but flattery, and their intolerance spread from politics into every other sphere. The result was that 'a reign of brutality and violence' set in over much of the country in mid-nineteenth-century America. Given this background, he conceded that Tocqueville had a point in his description of the facts as he saw them in the 1830s, but he was mistaken in supposing them essential to a democracy.[100]

Writing in the late Victorian years, Bryce saw enormous changes that convinced him of the recuperative powers of the American people. He argued that since the end of the Civil War education and culture had spread, religious bigotry had broken down, and socio-religious questions had been largely removed from politics. The passion and bitterness that marked the middle decades of the century had lessened; should they reappear in politics, they were likely to take on a new form. This was perceptive, but he was rather sanguine in believing that in the future there would be little attempt to repress the free exercise of opinion on issues outside mainstream politics. Bryce concluded that if his account were correct, 'the tyranny of the majority is no longer a blemish on the American system, and the charges brought against democracy from the supposed example of America are groundless'.[101]

* * *

As a British empiricist, Bryce recoiled from French sociology. When one of his friends asked him to include a chapter on the American theory of the state, he replied 'that the Americans had no theory of the state, and felt no need for one, being content, like the English, to base their constitutional ideas upon law and history'.[102] When pressed to provide some general views held by Americans about the role of government and its relationship to the individual, he listed what he called a few fundamental 'dogmas or maxims'. They might have been drawn from Benjamin Franklin or Thomas Paine, and included: the right of the individual to the enjoyment of his earnings, the right to free expression, the belief that political power derived from the people, the preference for local administration over central administration, and that government governed best when it governed least.[103]

In his chapter 'Laissez Faire', Bryce examined the last of these dogmas because it invited comparisons with Europe. Americans, he observed, generally wished to be left alone, to indulge their impulses and follow their stars. There was a common-sense assumption in the United States, based on the character and habits of the people, that everyone knew his own business best, that free enterprise made America prosperous, and that government interference did more harm than good. If canvassed, Bryce believed that nine out of ten Americans would tell a stranger that neither the State nor Federal governments interfered much in their lives and would ascribe the growth of the country to their self-reliant spirit. 'So far as there can be said to be any theory on the subject in a land which gets on without theories, *laissez aller* is the orthodox and accepted doctrine in the sphere both of Federal and State Legislation.'[104]

'Nevertheless the belief is groundless', Bryce asserted. In what he assumed would come as a surprise to his contemporaries and may come as one to his readers today, he argued that America was just as eager for state interference as England. He argued that no one need be shocked at this because civilization in the United States, as in Europe, was becoming more complex and threatening to the individual. Unlimited competition pressed hard on the weak, while the power of corporations and small groups of rich men in combination overshadowed the individual. The plutocrats abused their power and endangered the very freedom of association that men sought to secure by the law. The problems of industry and modernity told on the individual no less forcefully in the United States than in England, while Americans were even more impatient of delay. 'Having lived longer under a democratic government, the American masses have realized more perfectly than those of Europe that they are themselves the government.'[105] Consequently, they turned to it for relief.

Thus while Americans prided themselves on being devoted to *laissez-faire* in theory, Bryce believed that in practice they were as likely as the English to extend state action into ever-widening fields. Economic theory did not stop them because they were not a theoretical people; the sentiment of individualism did not stop them because government intervention usually took the form of protecting the many while restraining the few. 'So gradual has been the process of transition to this new habit that few but lawyers and economists have yet become aware of it, and the lamentations with which old-fashioned English thinkers accompany the march of legislation are in America scarcely heard and wholly unheeded.'[106]

While Bryce did not endorse an aggressive social policy for America, he was a man with a conscience, who would later support Campbell Bannerman's Liberal administration, which was notable for its social reforms. Unlike conservative commentators like Maine, who surveyed congressional legislation for signs of socialism, Bryce focused his research on State legislatures, where social experimentation was relatively easy. He discovered that the states were moving inexorably towards greater intervention. He provided various tables that presented a comparison of the legislation of six typical states, and Congress, along with British statutes bearing on the same topics. They included information on food and drink restrictions, railroad regulations, insurance companies and banks, and labour laws affecting women and children. 'In every one of these kinds of legislative interferences the Americans, at least the Western States, seem to have gone farther than the English Parliament.'[107]

Bryce hesitated to pronounce on the result of such legislation, but he asked whether the effects of it conformed to the expectations of the *laissez-faire* school of economists. 'Has the natural course of commerce and industry been disturbed, has the self-helpfulness of the citizen been weakened, has government done its work ill and a new door to jobbery been opened?' He took the view that some measures would succeed and others fail, but American states were pioneering new departures, serving the world by providing it with valuable data for instruction, which deserved greater attention. To Bryce, state legislators were 'unconscious philosophers', who experimented with more freedom and less risk than centralized countries like England or France. 'No people is shrewder than the American in perceiving when a law works ill, nor prompter in repealing it.'[108]

* * *

Bryce noted that no other country had tried a democratic form of government on such as scale as the United States, and those who thought that all civilized counties were moving towards democracy wished to know the answer to the question: 'How does Democracy answer?' He listed democracy's 'supposed faults', which included weakness in emergencies, instability, internal dissension, a frequent resort to violence, a desire to level down, a love of novelty, the tyranny of the majority, and ignorance that promoted demagoguery. He answered each charge in turn and concluded, rather brightly given the history of the United States, that only a couple of them had merit: the disposition to be lax in enforcing laws that were disliked by any large part of the population and the tendency to be indulgent to offenders.[109]

A more serious issue to Bryce was democracy's 'true faults'. He defined democracy not by revolution or equality but simply by majority rule. The rule of numbers meant the rule of ordinary citizens, who lacked training and were prey to the temptations of power. The direct rule of the multitude may become dangerous not only because of the normal failings and follies of human nature, but also because it is intellectually incompetent to conduct the daily work of government. For Bryce, the consequences of majority rule were a commonness of mind and tone, apathy among the leisured and learned classes, a want of judgement in the details of legislation, and laxity in the management of public business. Like Mill, he observed all of these tendencies in the United States.[110]

Of all the deficiencies of democracy that Bryce summarized, the most damning was the prominence of inferior men in politics. In short, Americans were ill served by their representatives. However good the people, they were not good enough to be able to dispense with capable and enlightened leaders. Bryce saw this fault of American democracy as the fruit 'of an optimism that underrated the inherent difficulties of politics and the failings of human nature, of a theory which has confused equality of civil rights and duties with equality of capacity, and of a thoughtlessness which has forgotten that the problems of the world and the dangers which beset society are always putting on new faces'.[111] The new spectre that worried Bryce was neither Toqueville's tyranny of the majority nor Bagehot's mob, but the growth of a plutocratic class, which used government as a means of private gain. 'Plutocracy, which the ancients contrasted with democracy, has shown in America an inauspicious affinity for certain professedly democratic institutions.'[112]

As Bryce saw it, Americans started their republic with a desire to prevent the abuse of power from Britain. They associated freedom with reducing the authority of legislatures and officials. No maxim was more potent than that which declared eternal vigilance to be the price of freedom. Unfortunately, American vigilance only took account of previous dangers and did not notice the emergence of new ones. 'Thus abuses were suffered to grow up, which seemed trivial in the midst of so general a prosperity; and good citizens who were occupied in other and more engrossing ways, allowed politics to fall into the hands of mean men.' Bryce concluded that no form of government required great leaders so much as a democracy. Amidst material prosperity,

Americans tended to lapse into a complacency that deadened aspiration. What they needed was 'to be thrilled by the emotions which great men can excite, stimulated by the ideals they present, stirred to a loftier sense of what national life may attain'.[113]

Bryce's technique was to follow every criticism with commensurate praise, so that every time he had America on the ropes he pulled his punches. For all the dangers presented by lacklustre leadership, the plutocracy, and the political machine, he remained optimistic. He did not fear the anarchy or the class struggle between labour and capital that beset Europe, for the private virtues of the people compensated for the failings of politics. One of the features of American life he most admired was its 'social equality', which to many Englishmen sounded odious, but which gave a naturalness and pleasantness to life that was a distinct advantage over Europe. Bryce had spent so much time among Americans over the years that he had lost any British hauteur that he might have had in favour of the charms of egalitarianism.[114] The combination of social equality and constitutional stability in the United States led him to look forward at the end of *The American Commonwealth* to a future 'not without anxiety... yet with a hope that is stronger than anxiety'.[115]

* * *

At the end of the Victorian era, Bryce remained sanguine about the 'essential unity of England and America'.[116] But when he turned his mind to Europe, the anxieties of a conservative broke through the progressive facade. While America prospered, Europe was entering what he called, in 1891, 'An Age of Discontent'. Even Britain was not exempt from censure, for it had reached an almost pure form of democracy under a monarchy, and there was 'hardly a limb or joint, so to speak, of our Constitution which is not threatened'.[117] For Bryce, like Maine, an eighteenth-century written Constitution had provided equilibrium and political stability in the United States, while a malleable, unwritten Constitution had created imbalances and instability in Britain. On reading Bryce's great encomium to the conservative nature of American democracy, Lord Acton remarked: 'I descry a bewildered whig emerging from the third volume with a reverent appreciation of ancestral wisdom, Burke's "Reflections"... and a growing belief in the function of ghosts to make laws for the quick.'[118]

6

Conclusion

Anglo-American Exceptionalism

> If half the exertions were made to prepare the minds of the majority for the place they are about to take in their own government, which are made for the chimerical purpose of preventing them from assuming that place, mankind would purchase at a cheap price safety from incalculable evils, and the benefit of a government indefinitely improvable.
>
> (John Stuart Mill, 1835)

> America illustrates even more clearly than France the truth...that pure democracy is one of the least representative of governments. In hardly any other country does the best life and energy of the nation flow so habitually apart from politics.
>
> (William Edward Hartpole Lecky, 1896)

The American and French Revolutions sparked the most serious thinking on the nature of politics in Britain since the seventeenth century. Few issues escaped the attention of Victorian thinkers on American democracy, from the US Constitution to its practical application, from the Supreme Court to spoils, from slavery to the suffrage. While such matters precipitated discussion, they were often seen against the background of British politics, which was undergoing a seismic shift in the aftermath of the crisis surrounding the passing of the 1832 Reform Act. The transfer of power symbolized by the Act was a shock to the system, whatever an individual's allegiances. Increasingly, Victorian thinkers were highly sensitive to the changing political landscape on both sides of the Atlantic; their purpose was not simply to survey the democratic terrain but also to shape it in keeping with their principles.

In the battle of political ideas, the big idea addressed by the Victorians was the nature of democracy itself, which had exercised the western imagination since the Greeks. Like Tocqueville, they saw the intellectual debate in the light of aristocratic traditions. But unlike Tocqueville, Mill, Bagehot, Maine, and Bryce were not born into the landed aristocracy. (Bryce, who was raised to the peerage, was the most positive about democracy.) Whatever their social origins, all of them felt they were part of a new era in the study of politics, in which a fundamental issue was the shifting balance of power from aristocratic to popular government. For those thinkers who saw America as predictive of the future—and few did not—the United States was, as Tocqueville insisted, the greatest test of democracy in history. But with the reduction in the power of the House of Lords in 1911 and advent of universal suffrage in 1918 the test ended in Britain, and the debate over democracy inspired by America in the nineteenth century subsided.

It may be tempting to say that Victorian commentators simply provided a gloss on Tocqueville. This would be mistaken. They all read *Democracy in America*, but as often as not they found fault with it. This partly had to do with ideological differences and partly to do with Tocqueville's analysis, which, for all its speculative genius, bore many of the hallmarks of the 1830s. As Bryce remarked in the 1880s, many of the evils that the Frenchman observed had vanished while new ones had emerged.[1] Mill was the most admiring of *Democracy in America*, but even he dissented from many of its ideas. Bagehot, Maine, and Bryce were less admiring and challenged Tocqueville's theories, from the inevitability of democracy to the potential of the majority to tyrannize the public. All of them added substance and weight to the debate over popular government, which intensified as the implications of expanding the suffrage began to loom larger in the second half of the nineteenth century.

A message that resounds through the British writing on American government—from Burke to Bentham, from Mill to Maine, from Bagehot to Bryce—was that the United States took its political inspiration from the mother country. History is fate. For the British, Lincoln's 'mystic cords of memory' from the Revolution did not excise those mystic chords of colonial history that had reverberated through America since the first English settlers landed in Jamestown. Colonial rule lasted for nearly two centuries before American independence. The fifty-five delegates who attended the Constitutional Convention in 1787 were overwhelmingly of English ancestry—six had attended universities in Britain.[2] The great majority of them had served in the colonial legislatures where they exercised a goodly measure of self-government; and while they looked broadly for their political ideas, they agreed that Britain had the best available constitution on which to build a new nation. This was the background against which the American exceptionalist school of thought sought a divorce from its colonial past.

Across the Atlantic, there was widespread agreement over the intellectual origins of the American government.[3] In British eyes, as one authority noted, the US Constitution 'has consistently been seen as an adaptation, more or less successful, and at least in some degree necessary, of British Whig constitutional notions and established English and colonial practice'.[4] Mill assumed that the republican Constitution, though bound to govern differently, was indebted to the mother country; and it was more likely to be effective if it continued many of the practices that had long existed in Britain.[5] Bagehot dismissed the US Constitution as a political straitjacket, but attributed what little good he found in it to British precedent and Anglo-Saxon respect for the law. Maine cherished the straitjacket but insisted that the eighteenth-century British Constitution served as the original for the former colonists, with a few modifications introduced by new circumstances. To Bryce, a conservative English spirit, in keeping with Whig principles, infused the American Commonwealth.

Dicey, the legal theorist who had travelled to America with Bryce, powerfully reinforced such views in his seminal *Introduction to the Study of the Law of the Constitution* (1885): 'The institutions of America are in their spirit little else than a gigantic development of the ideas which lie at the basis of the political and legal institutions of England.'[6] In *Democracy and Liberty* (1896), the Irish historian William Lecky, a liberal in politics but suspicious of democracy, noted how closely the aims and standards of the men who framed the Constitution of 1787 resembled those of eighteenth-century English statesmen. The Americans had a different framework but the same purposes, which, to Lecky, were essentially conservative: 'To divide and restrict power; to secure property; to check the appetite for organic change; to guard individual liberty against the tyranny of the multitude, as well as against the tyranny of an individual or class;

CONCLUSION: ANGLO-AMERICAN EXCEPTIONALISM

to infuse into American political life a spirit of continuity and of sober and moderate freedom.'[7]

* * *

The impact of Victorian constitutional writers on American opinion is difficult to judge. Mill, Bagehot, Maine, and Bryce all received notices in the press and reviews in the periodical literature of their day. Their books eventually appeared in university courses. But apart from Bryce, whose *American Commonwealth* was widely distributed, there is little evidence that they reached a broad audience. Democracies do not take kindly to censure, and Americans often feel it is their patriotic duty to invite praise and ignore criticism, especially foreign criticism. But academics and intellectuals, particularly in the Northeast, often nodded in agreement with the Victorian critics. By the end of the nineteenth century, leading American authorities on the US Constitution, among them Woodrow Wilson, Henry Jones Ford, and Charles Ellis Stevens, broadly endorsed many of the views of their British counterparts. They indulged in what has been called selective Victorianism, taking what suited them and disregarding what did not. They took more from Mill and Bryce than Bagehot and Maine.

Most notably, late nineteenth-century American authorities generally accepted the derivative nature of the US government, which marked a break with the exceptionalist tradition of scholarship that saw the Constitution providing a unique system of government, independent of British precedent.[8] In *Congressional Government* (1885), Woodrow Wilson, a devotee of Bagehot, took it as obvious that the Convention of 1787 was made up of men of the 'English-speaking race', who took the system of government with which they were familiar and adapted it.[9] Stevens, who thanked Maine for his assistance in the preface of his *Sources of the Constitution of the United States* (1894), remarked: 'The Constitution of the United States...does not stand in historical isolation....It looks back to the annals of the colonies and of the motherland for its sources and its explanation.'[10] Ford, who cited Bagehot, Bryce, and Lecky in his influential *The Rise and Growth of American Politics* (1898), thought it obvious that the American government 'patterned its behavior as closely as possible to the English style'.[11]

British influence thus propelled the Anglo-Saxon or 'Teutonic' school of interpretation, which, as Charles Beard noted, posed a serious challenge to the exceptionalist tradition promoted earlier in the century.[12] As Stevens remarked, there were still some in the United States who were unwilling to look to England for the foundation of their institutions, 'but surely Americanism can never be more truly American' than when accepting the fact that the United States is a 'progression from the Anglo-Teutonic past'.[13] Would the US government, he might have added, have taken the same form had the French won the Seven Years War, or had the Spanish been the colonial power? How many constitutions, and of what character, would have been drafted had the French ruled North America? How many caudillos would have surfaced had the Spanish ruled? Those who see the United States as a unique political experiment without reference to tradition or colonial origins avoid such questions. Despite the propaganda to the contrary, the Puritan John Winthrop fashioned his 'City upon a Hill' in the hills of Suffolk, England, not the hills of Massachusetts.[14]

The growing American belief in a historically rooted Anglo-Saxon Constitution worked to undermine the exceptionalist tradition of scholarship; but it did little, if anything, to undermine the Constitution's claim to other-worldly, religious devotion. The heyday of Anglo-Saxonism in the late nineteenth century was also an era of Constitutional reverence in the United States. The link between the exceptionalist school of history and worship of the Constitution was perhaps weaker than might be imagined. The American 'providential' tradition could incorporate a British presence, if only as a prelude to the faith, rather like Christianity building on a Jewish foundation. Here, Bryce may be seen as a touchstone, perhaps even an influence, for he approved of the American worship of the Constitution, while seeing the origins of the document in Britain. Accepting constitutional associations with the mother country did not, as Stevens suggested, prevent Anglo-Saxon Americans from praising themselves.

The idea that America stood outside history rarely entered the minds of British commentators, who saw the break with Britain as conditional, not absolute. (Lord Acton, who thought the American Revolution a unique event, was a notable exception.[15]) To them, the bonds of kinship, language, and law remained unbroken despite the Revolution, the War of 1812, and recurring diplomatic tensions. Indeed, for many nineteenth-century American commentators, the nation's British inheritance—its mores and habits of mind, its respect for the law and representative government—were determinant. 'Say what you will', observed Harriet Beecher Stowe in a letter home from Liverpool in 1853, 'an American, particularly a New Englander, can never approach the old country without a kind of thrill and pulsation of kindred. Its history for two centuries was our history. Its literature, laws, and language are our literature, laws, and language.... Our very life-blood is English life-blood.'[16] This was a point of view that Englishmen admired in their American cousins, even when they dismissed them as provincials.

Provincials or not, Americans remained predominantly Anglo-Saxon in their attitudes in the first century of the republic. Even today there are those who argue that cultural diversity simply cloaks the underlying Britishness of American values.[17] The religion, manners, and morals of most Americans continued to mirror those of the mother country in the Victorian years, which to both Britons and Americans was often a point of pride. President Lincoln, in a letter of condolence to Queen Victoria on the death of Prince Albert, said that 'the People of the United States are kindred of the People of Great Britain. With all our distinct national interests, objects, and aspirations, we are conscious that our moral strength is largely derived from that relationship.'[18] 'Anglo-Saxonism' dated to the seventeenth century but grew in intensity after the divisions over the Civil War dissipated.[19] By the 1880s the term had broken through the confines of race and stood as often as not for 'a civilization, for ideas and institutions, originating indeed with a certain ethnic type of mankind, but no longer its exclusive property'.[20]

To a remarkable degree, British writers on democracy were advocates of a special transatlantic relationship based on Anglo-Saxonism, a position widely endorsed by their American counterparts by the end of the nineteenth century. Among many others, Mill, Bagehot, Maine, and Bryce all assumed that the English-speaking people had a genius for self-government ripened by experience, which set them apart from less favoured nations. As Woodrow Wilson remarked, they came to their democracies '*through habit*', unlike other peoples who rushed prematurely into democracy through 'impatience'.[21] As proof, Anglo-Saxons had only to look at the Spanish colonies in the New World, which compared so unfavourably with North America. Bagehot, it may be recalled, thought America's English origins spared it from Spanish 'imbecility'.[22] Maine also cast a censorious Anglo-Saxon gaze at Spain and its colonies and counted scores of serious military uprisings 'in most of which the mob took part'.[23]

Americans often put the Anglo-Saxon case just as emphatically. Senator Albert Beveridge of Indiana said 'God has not been preparing the English-speaking and Teutonic peoples for a thousand years for nothing.... No! He has made us master organizers of the world to establish system where chaos reigns.'[24] William Evarts, the Secretary of State, gave Anglo-Saxonism a curious twist for a man with presidential ambitions in a speech at the centennial celebration to mark the Battle of Bennington in 1878: 'I believe... had Queen Victoria been on the throne, instead of George III, or if we had postponed our rebellion until Queen Victoria reigned, it would not have been necessary, and had there been any rebellion at all, it would have been on the part of England.'[25] At the time of the Queen's Golden Jubilee in 1887, the Revd C. I. Scofield of Dallas, Texas, spoke for Anglo-Saxons across America in his declaration that 'we are part of Great Britain—that earth-encircling family of English speaking nations the planting and nurture of which is the most remarkable of God's modern miracles'.[26]

It was telling that the usage 'Victorian' became a commonplace in nineteenth-century America. Apart from the Irish communities, admiration for Queen Victoria was seemingly boundless in the United States, where she was hailed for her role in spreading Anglo-Saxon civilization, with its consoling narrative of constitutional rectitude, social decorum, and Protestantism. The tributes from across the Atlantic began with her accession in 1837, continued at her coronation the following year, and reached a crescendo during the American centennial celebrations.[27] By the time of her Silver Jubilee in 1887, she had an iconic status on both sides of the Atlantic, which reflected the tenor of Anglo-American relations. In the New York celebrations to honour the Queen, a former mayor of the City observed that 'Great Britain and America now see how the tangled threads of Anglo-Saxon greatness have become the warp and woof of human progress over a large portion of the globe.... The two nations have had their differences; but behind them all beat, as I believe, two kindred hearts.'[28]

For all the kindred spirit, misunderstandings were inevitable whenever an older, aristocratic culture came into contact with a younger, egalitarian one. Most British commentators were elitists struggling with populism, which limited their impact in the United States where ideas of popular sovereignty prevailed. With the exception of Bryce, who knew America best, they felt little sympathy for the masses. The more they focused on high politics, the more likely they were to give precedence to the culture of the governing elite rather than the intellectual and moral tone of the governed. Victorian commentators had imbibed more of Burke than Paine, who rarely entered their discussions. They found the advocates of the American Demos rough around the edges and feared a descent into vulgarity. Americans, in turn, disliked being patronized by supercilious Britons, a complaint famously expressed in James Russell Lowell's 'On a Certain Condescension in Foreigners' (1871).

The British eventually came to terms with the emergent power of the United States and the growing sophistication of their transatlantic cousins. At the time Bryce and Maine were writing on US politics in the 1880s, the population of the United States surpassed Britain's. Given America's growing share of world markets and widening sphere of influence, it was becoming much more difficult to see its citizens as English provincials, as Mill and Bagehot had done, or '*queer* English people', as the English actress Fanny Kemble called them in the mid-nineteenth century.[29] But history and language remained decisive. With the years, British visitors to the US were more likely to see America as a nation of great diversity, but essentially English in its culture. In turn, many Americans, with the confidence of maturity, looked to Britain for a reciprocal regard born out of language, history, and shared interests.

For Mill, Bagehot, and Bryce, the end of slavery represented an important turning point in their attitudes towards the United States, for it invigorated their sense of kinship with Americans. In the late Victorian years, more positive feelings shaped relations between Britain and the United States, fostered by transatlantic family ties, intermarriage between important families, and mutual respect for Queen Victoria.[30] Despite the growing diversity of American ancestry, the spread of Anglo-Saxon civilization had become part of the cultural conversation, which provided a rationale for improvements between the two countries. Anglo-Americanism may be seen as a hybrid, transatlantic form of exceptionalism, which brought the British and the Americans into a society of mutual admiration compatible with the nationalism of both countries. One may look to Victorian thinkers on American democracy to see the special relationship between Britain and the United States taking shape, however strained by touchiness, apprehension, and misunderstanding.

In the latter decades of the nineteenth century, Britons and Americans increasingly saw the rule of law and the liberty of the individual as the supreme contributions of the English-speaking people and assumed that they had a special mission in the world based on blood, culture, and their capacity for self-government.[31] Bryce's analysis confirmed that the US Constitution enshrined the supremacy of the law, and that the interplay of federal and state authorities under the umbrella of the courts produced a remarkably stable, indeed conservative, democracy. As he and many others of his generation saw it, American constitutionalism was the consummation of the English common law tradition. Some of them assumed that the United States, for all her revolutionary origins, had become a mirror image of England, a view reinforced by a Constitution that remained largely unchanged as an instrument of governance since the eighteenth century. As Dicey wrote to Bryce in 1884: 'Is it not a mistake to consider the U.S. a new country at all'?[32]

In an article in the *Contemporary Review* in 1897, Dicey took the idea of Anglo-Saxon unity to what might be deemed its logical conclusion. Like other commentators, he applied a linguistic test of nationhood and was inclined to think that anyone who spoke English as the mother tongue had the right to be called English.[33] Thus he proposed a common citizenship for all Englishmen and Americans, what he dubbed 'isopolity' for the 'English Race'. The romantic idea was straightforward but impractical given the bureaucratic niceties of nation states in an era of mass emigration from disparate parts of the globe. Irish Americans, not to mention other ethnic groups, would have been startled by the proposal

> that England and the United States should, by concurrent and appropriate legislation, create such a common citizenship, or, to put the matter in a more concrete and therefore in a more intelligible form, that an Act of the Imperial Parliament should make every citizen of the United States, during the continuance of peace between England and America, a British subject, and that simultaneously an Act of Congress should make every British subject... a Citizen of the United States.[34]

* * *

If Americans will always have the British with them, the reverse is also true. The belief that Europe was coming under the spell of US democracy aroused many a British writer from an aristocratic slumber. In an era of democratic fervour, the New World threatened the establishment of the Old. Comparisons with the United States could be unsettling for Britons, whether they feared or favoured egalitarianism. Equality had justice on its side but lacked the charm and brilliance of aristocracy. What agitated Mill, Bagehot, Bryce, and Maine, among other Victorians, was that Britain was moving towards a mass democracy with consequences that were dreary and unpredictable. They recognized the stability of the American Constitution but found the British one undergoing a vexing transformation. It had gone through so many changes that it would have been barely recognizable even to the constitutionalist George III.

Democracy was on the rise, albeit unevenly across Europe, and British thinkers often expressed a dividedness of mind about it. Apart from Bryce, they saw little charm in egalitarianism. Classless America was not very compelling to men accustomed to social distinctions, who tended to translate 'equality of condition' into mediocrity. They admired America's freedoms, but dismissed its culture for lacking a leisured class of independent thinkers. They applauded America's enterprise but found its leaders feeble and its citizens coarse. They praised the US Constitution, but worried about its departures from parliamentary government. They respected the Founding Fathers, who shared their view of human nature, but thought of them as Englishmen displaced. Ironically, they dismissed Americans as conformists and provincials, but praised them for being Anglo-Saxon conformists and provincials.

The caveats about American society, though often severe, were understandable given that the British commentators came from an aristocratic society, and one that provided the most stable and successful political culture in Europe. When Bagehot saw the British franchise extended in 1867, he feared the mob. When Maine saw it further extended in 1884, he contemplated national ruin. Few philosophers had trumpeted democracy in the past—certainly not the authors of the *Federalist*—and the aristocratic Tocqueville himself sent out mixed signals about its effects. He ended the second volume of *Democracy in America*, after all, with the warning that social equality might lead to 'servitude', 'barbarism', and 'misery'. Maine's fear that democracy would lead to 'death' simply carried Tocqueville's anxieties to an extreme.

* * *

Tocqueville had called for 'a new political science' to address the problems of 'a world altogether new'.[35] Whether nineteenth-century

British writers on American democracy can be said to be 'scientists' is questionable, though such claims could be made for Bryce, the Gradgrind empiricist.[36] In any case, the Victorians provided a probing analysis that was missing in the United States, where criticism of the Constitution paled in comparison to interpretations of it by the legal priesthood. The British expressed a detachment free from the pieties of American writers, but they failed to free themselves from seeing the US government through British eyes. The more they applauded America as the offspring of the mother country, the more they were inclined to promote Anglo-Saxon unity. Bryce, who was arguably the least speculative British authority on American government and certainly the most encyclopedic, could not escape from a sentimental attachment to the English-speaking peoples, nor did he wish to.

If nationalism and a tendency to self-congratulation blinded Americans to the colonial origins of their political system, history and a tendency to self-congratulation blinded the British to what was unique about America. With an inordinate sense of their own superiority, the English had difficulty in recognizing that America was not England.[37] Moreover, to cede great originality to the US form of government would have been a betrayal of Anglo-American unity. When Bryce, who was more worldly than most of his fellow countrymen, hailed the American Commonwealth he was paying tribute to the British Commonwealth that nurtured it. In so doing he challenged the assumption that American democracy was creating a world 'altogether new'. Newness was not the distinguishing feature of American government to those who believed the origins of democracy were to be found in England. Like others before him, Bryce insisted that the Founding Fathers were not radicals but the heirs of Magna Carta and 1688. As he saw it, Runnymede, like Philadelphia, could make a claim to being 'the birthplace of democracy'.[38]

For all the talk about the origins of democracy, British commentators had grown up with a post-1688 hereditary aristocracy and widely accepted a degree of social hierarchy, in which an elite was educated to rule. They assumed that democracies, like aristocracies, required men of superior ability to provide stable, efficient government. Many of them had a fondness for Carlyle's great man theory, which had a particular resonance for them in the American context. Apart from Lincoln, they did not find any great leaders after the generation of the Founding Fathers; and given the nature of electoral politics in the United States

CONCLUSION: ANGLO-AMERICAN EXCEPTIONALISM 133

they were not sanguine that there were any waiting in the wings. Mill, Bagehot, and Maine dismissed most American presidents as mediocrities; Bryce, as noted, called them 'intellectual pigmies'. Defenders of Tyler, Polk, Taylor, Fillmore, Pierce, Buchanan, Johnson, and other American leaders might dismiss these charges as the prejudices of men born into an aristocracy; but the British insisted that it was the nature of a specifically American democracy that discouraged men of genius from entering the political arena. As they insisted, the United States did not have the Constitution to thank for its great presidents.

This view of the downside of American democracy was widespread in Britain, where there was greater pride in the capacity of national leaders. The English man of letters Leslie Stephen, who visited America during the Civil War, expressed the conventional opinion that the inducements to political service in a young, practical country with competing forms of government were relatively small.[39] Goldwin Smith agreed, adding that Americans were a 'rough people' without a culture or a past.[40] Mill did not see the decline of American politicians as a result of constitutional limits on power; rather he saw the trend as a reflection of the electorate, the 'mechanical nature' of government and a function of circumstance.[41] Bagehot noted that a system of competing sovereignties did not stir noble ambition and made running for office hardly worth the effort for men of ability. There was a general view that great men emerged to meet national emergencies—witness Lincoln—and that men of distinction were not often required in America with its natural advantages and want of foreign enemies. Ordinary times produced ordinary men.

With an air of superiority, the Victorians saw a combination of ill-educated voters and a defective electoral system producing inferior men in American government. As Maine put it, even when American leaders were eloquent they were 'manifestly listening nervously at one end of a speaking-tube which receives at its other end the suggestions of a lower intelligence'.[42] Most British commentators took a dim view of the common man as voter—at home or abroad—and feared the spread of democratic vulgarity.'We must educate our masters' observed the MP Robert Lowe after the 1867 Reform Act added a million working men to the British electorate.[43] In America, the suffrage had been extended to white males decades earlier, with results that left many British writers perplexed. But few of them dissented from the Fifteenth Amendment, ratified in 1870 but not fully realized for nearly a century, which stipulated that the right of citizens to vote could not be denied because of 'race, color, or previous condition of servitude'. Given the hesitant progress of democratic reform on both sides of the Atlantic, electoral systems and popular education preoccupied British thinkers.

The British assumed that the want of great men in public life left the country vulnerable to the corrupting influences of American democracy. Elections created party intrigues and momentary bursts of passion, with unhappy consequences when candidates set aside the interest of the state as they ran to meet the caprices of the electorate.[44] Though familiar with the warnings about factionalism in the *Federalist* and in Washington's farewell address, Tocqueville and Mill did not stress the danger of a party system that would ultimately overshadow and threaten republican governance. When they were writing about America in the 1830s, political parties were relatively small and the spoils system in its infancy. The structure that shaped their studies of America had more to do with the contrast between aristocracy and democracy than factionalism. But in reaction to the growth of parties, Mill stepped up his criticism of electoral abuses in *Considerations on Representative Government*.

As the party tendrils reached ever more deeply into city and state governments after the Civil War, British commentators took an increasingly ominous view of American politics, which they saw as irrational and ramshackle. They regularly commented on the poor candidates and the number and frequency of elections, which encouraged vulgarity and volatility in public life. A mischief that every British critic found in American politics was the incessant campaigning, the relentless cycle of indifference punctuated by intervals of partisan passion. By the time Maine and Bryce were writing in the 1880s, electioneering was in luxuriant bloom, while issues rarely broke through the surface. Principle had largely given way to spoils. The first purpose of the contending parties was to secure office and divide the perquisites of power among their partisans. The quality of candidates was secondary to winning. The result was a corrupted, deracinated politics that inhibited effective governance.

Arguably, Maine and Bryce provided the most trenchant critiques of the American party system in the nineteenth century.[45] One might see them as carrying forward the arguments of Madison, who had depicted factionalism as an endemic threat to representative government. Americans had failed to still the anxieties of the *Federalist* papers about organized parties—those wilful, combative minorities—that pursued their sectarian interests against the spirit of the Founding Fathers. Washington had warned that over time parties might 'become potent engines, by which cunning, ambitious, and unprincipled men will be enabled to subvert the power of the people, and to usurp for themselves the reins of government; destroying afterwards the very engines, which have lifted them to unjust dominion'.[46] According to Maine and Bryce, the time of 'unjust dominion' had arrived in America.

The iconoclastic Maine, not one to miss an opportunity to ridicule democracy, attacked party politics as part of his wider attack on popular government. For him, democratic politics was combative, what Henry Adams would later call 'the systematic organization of hatreds'.[47] Belligerence was its essence: 'It is war without the city transmuted to war within the city, but mitigated in the process.'[48] The best historical justification that Maine could offer for the American party system was that it prevented political rivals from killing one another. He took the view that the Founding Fathers were unprepared for the rapid development of parties and expected the contrivances of the Federal Constitution to defeat any evil influences that might arise. But corruption soon sprang into vigorous life with greater prosperity, population growth, and diffused electoral power with the widening of the franchise.

British writers, like American ones, often pointed an accusatory finger at Andrew Jackson for the practice 'to the victor the spoils'. In *Democracy and Liberty*, Lecky said that Jackson inaugurated a system of spoils that 'spread like a leprosy over all political life'.[49] Increasingly, the competing parties adopted the principle of replacing officials who did not belong to their factions with those who did. Lecky cited American figures on the army of Federal employees who had little to recommend them apart from connection and backroom deals. By the administration of President Cleveland in the 1880s, the number of public servants dismissed for political ends reached nearly 100,000. As Lecky put it, 'office was the coin in which to pay political debts and gain the services of political *condottieri*'.[50] Jobbery and corrupt practices encouraged the tendency of American politicians to see the distribution of sweeteners and pork as keys to power.

As a consequence of increasing political corruption, many a candidate saw the enemy in the mirror and ran on an anti-government platform, which the Federal structure of competing sovereignties invigorated. America had devised a political system in which politicians benefited from opposing the government in Washington, while exploiting its privileges and perquisites. They were content to eat pork and give it away. Furthermore, as the nation expanded and the number of public offices grew, plutocrats and others with an interest in government policy spent ever increasing sums of money in what Maine called the 'wholesale bribery' of officialdom.[51] As Bryce argued, the American moneyed class had an unhealthy fondness for democratic institutions. With the emergence of lobbyists and party bosses, many American politicians came to believe that the electoral system could not survive without corruption. It was reminiscent of eighteenth-century English politics, when votes and parliamentary seats were bought and sold. But unlike America, Britain had instituted reforms by handing over patronage to the Civil Service Commissioners and passing the Corrupt Practices Act (1883), which restrained election expenditure.

Combative parties, plutocratic lobbying, electoral corruption, the spoils system, feeble candidates, and lacklustre presidents were among the chief criticisms British commentators made of American democracy in the Victorian years. All these complaints had merit, but arguably, as Bryce observed, they were not the most serious faults of democracy. Majority rule meant the rule of ordinary people, who wanted the perquisites of power but lacked the intellectual capacity and training to govern. As Tocqueville discovered, America was a materialistic society that had many ambitious men but few lofty ambitions, and political power was becoming concentrated in their hands. In a sense, the tyranny of the majority turned on the tyranny of incompetent leaders elected by dulled and distracted citizens with low expectations of government. Lecky argued that in America the tyranny of the majority rarely assumed a more odious form than when elected officials were 'the tools of a faction or a mob'.[52]

Majority rule was an issue on which the British ruminated with a high degree of unanimity and not without anxiety. For Mill, American democracy, for all its promise, threatened to debase the political culture, with the uninspiring leading the uninspired. For Bagehot, constitutional checks and balances led to political inertia, which made government the playground of embittered hacks. For Maine, the 'Age of Progress' was a fiction; legislative zeal and political innovation would simply lead to decay, buoyed by a superstitious public given to amnesia and incapable of effective remedies. For Bryce, the most positive of British commentators on America, majority rule resulted in a commonness of mind, apathy among the educated classes, and laxity in the management of public business. A weakness of American democracy was the other side of American optimism, which confused equality of rights with the equality of capacity, while underrating the difficulties of politics and the failings of human nature.

Much of the Victorian debate over democracy turned on the unresolved tension between liberty and equality. It was an issue that had captivated political theorists for centuries, but which was given new resonance by the surge of democracy in America. Americans themselves took pride in the absence of rank in the United States and boasted that their liberty was more complete than elsewhere because equality was blended into it. For those like Maine, who insisted that distinctions of rank were inevitable, liberty and equality were mutually exclusive. Bryce noted the American worship of wealth, dynastic families, and social distinctions, but he asserted that there was no rank in America that entitled any individual to special consideration. Though impressed by the Constitution's prohibition on titles of nobility, he recognized that grades and distinctions were widespread and led to social exclusiveness, if not political privilege.[53] He would not have been surprised by the rise of the Roosevelts, the Tafts, the Kennedys, and the Bushes.

Most British commentators described America as a land of equality. But like Tocqueville, they worried that equality promoted conformity and a soft despotism that stupefied a people and stifled dissent. As Mill saw it, the greatest hope for the cause of liberty lay in the civic engagement of an educated public.[54] Democratic citizens wanted both to be led and to be free. But the price of liberty, as Bryce argued, was the primacy of duties over rights.[55] It required the habit of civic association and a measure of self-government, what the Founding Fathers would have called republican spirit or virtue. Mill applied this thought to politics: 'Only by the habit of superintending their local interests can that diffusion of intelligence and mental activity...take place among the mass of a people, which can qualify them to superintend with steadiness or consistency the proceedings of their government.'[56] The only check on 'political slavery', he wrote in *Principles of Political Economy*, was the check maintained over governors by the voluntary activity of the governed.[57]

But keeping the American government in check was, as Bryce said, a labour of Sisyphus in a nation with a distracted electorate and a large number of disparate states pulling in different directions. A fault of democracy may be summed up in Daniel Defoe's unhappy proverb: 'Everybody's business is Nobody's business'. At the foundation of the Republic, some thinkers thought the size and complexity of America would encourage lethargy and erode participatory citizenship. The Anti-Federalist 'Brutus', who opposed the draft Constitution in 1787, had made a powerful, though unpersuasive, argument: 'a free republic cannot succeed over a country of such immense extent, containing such a number of inhabitants, and these encreasing [sic] in such rapid progression as that of the whole United States'.[58] He cited Montesquieu no less as his authority, and in his day there were only thirteen states and a population of only about four million.

History furnished no example of a 'free republic' as large as the United States. Nor was the cause of American democracy aided by the distrust of the distant government in Washington, which, as Bagehot and Bryce noted, was deeply ingrained in the culture of the United States. Nor was it aided by the entrenched party rivalries that undermined the relations between the Presidency and the Congress. Nor was it aided by the Constitution predicated on competing sovereignties, which, immune to criticism and hard to amend, impeded change. Nor was it aided by a Federal system, which undermined the central government's response to a crisis, whether manmade or natural. Dicey, like Bagehot before him, argued that federalism created an elaborate subdivision of powers that was not conducive to stable or effective government. Americans, as he put it, 'must desire union, and must not desire unity'.[59]

Bagehot believed that ageing countries outgrow the constitutional clothes of their youth. As Rousseau had put it in the *Social Contract*: 'A body which is too big for its constitution collapses and perishes, crushed by its own weight.'[60] Americans, however, saw their formal Constitution fitting all sizes, a point of view that bemused the British, who tended to prefer the tailoring of their own Constitution. Maine, the most reactionary critic of democracy, was an exception. He disparaged the Victorian parliamentary system because it had become too loose and liberal, accommodating change too readily. In contrast, he praised the US government because it was made conservatively, inhibiting expansive legislation, which he took to be the besetting sin of democracies. For Maine and Bryce, it was a measure of American conservatism that an eighteenth-century document continued to shape—and to control—the nation's politics given the massive social change and the turbulence of public opinion. For Mill and Bagehot, writing against the backdrop of the Civil War, it was a measure of the good sense of the American public that such a flawed Constitution worked at all.

* * *

In *Democracy and Liberty*, written at the close of the nineteenth century, Lecky lucidly summarized much of what his fellow British commentators had earlier observed about the United States. Like Tocqueville, Mill, Bagehot, Maine, and Bryce, whose works he studied and cited, he saw America as a favoured nation, a bastion of democracy—and politically flawed. As a Burkean, he admired the US Constitution because it limited the possibilities of misgovernment. As a student of eighteenth-century England, he noted how the framers of the US Constitution mirrored the aims of Georgian statesmen, which contributed to the exceptional, transatlantic character of the American government. But he abhorred the unique profligacy of American politics, the spoils system, the jobbing candidates, the pusillanimous leaders, and the mass of ignorant voters who followed them like sheep.'No feature of American life strikes a stranger so powerfully as the extraordinary indifference...with which notorious frauds and notorious corruption in the sphere of politics are viewed by American public opinion.'[61]

For all the corruption and political cynicism, Lecky noted the good nature of the American people, who so often greeted the profligacy of public life with 'little more than a disdainful smile'.[62] Tocqueville had applauded the buoyancy of the American people and observed that equality in democracies propelled the idea of man's perfectibility, whereas class hierarchy in aristocracies put a limit on such ideas.[63] Likewise, British commentators often remarked on the prevailing optimism in the United States, which led Americans to have hope for the future even when anxious about the present. As Lecky saw it, Americans had a naive belief that ultimately the 'survival of the fittest' would come into play and 'that in the course of time, and after prolonged and costly experiences, the turbid element of corruption will clarify, and its worst constituents sink like sediment to the bottom'.[64]

Lecky believed that historians, who judged from past examples, might be pessimistic about the future of a country governed by mediocrities, where corruption was rampant and reform unlikely. To him, the United States had survived and prospered partly because of its extraordinary natural advantages, but largely—and here was a delicious twist—because the nation's best and brightest remained 'apart from politics'. Perhaps the lack of interest in politics by the educated—Mill's learned and leisured classes—was not as harmful to democracy as British critics had long suggested. Lecky noted the paradox of a great nation that teemed with energy, intelligence, and moral excellence allowing itself to be so badly governed. But then he did not overrate the role of politics in America. Life was elsewhere for a restless people with livings to make and a continent to subdue. After all the British anxiety about popular government, Lecky concluded, with a sigh of relief, that 'pure democracy is one of the least representative of governments'.[65]

* * *

In the twentieth century, Britain's power waned and the United States replaced it as the world's leading nation. Just how much the ascendancy of America can be explained by its written Constitution is moot. Britain, after all, did quite well without one, though a more elastic Constitution did not prevent its decline. The American Constitution has served as a binding force, has encouraged commerce, has protected property, and in its unruly fashion has provided the wherewithal for the peaceful transfer of power, essential in a working democracy. But was the nation's prosperity and success best ascribed to the excellence of its Constitution, to its natural advantages, or to the character of its people, whom the British regarded as kith and kin? While Americans trumpeted their Constitution as pivotal, the British tended to emphasize national character and natural advantage.

American reverence for their written Constitution is arguably a triumph of faith over experience. As Maine would say, it reflected a triumph of the historical principle over the democratic one. Contrary to popular prejudice, the framers did not seek to create a democracy in 1787, which they associated with anarchy and corruption, but to secure the survival of the Union. Neither side at the Constitutional Convention thought they were engaged in a struggle for 'democracy'.[66] They fashioned an eighteenth-century republic that required the expression of civic virtue and restraints on party factionalism to flourish. As the nation became a 'democratic republic' in the nineteenth century, history justified their anxieties about popular government and the perils of partisanship. Arguably, the British saw this more clearly than Americans, whose devotion at the Constitutional altar discouraged normal 'observational' methods.

The Founding Fathers would probably be surprised by the veneration with which the Constitution is treated today by those who worship its every clause and comma. They recognized that they had produced an imperfect instrument of governance, beset by compromise and issues left unresolved. Less than a century later, it could not avert the bloodiest war in American history—against fellow Americans. But by then, decades of propaganda had worked their spell, and it was seen, as Washington hoped, as a great charter, the principal pillar of the nation's independence and liberty.[67] As Bryce prophetically observed in the 1880s, reverence for the 'beloved' document had 'become so potent a conservative influence, that no proposal of fundamental change seems likely to be entertained'.[68] Nor has it.

The American Constitution, as it has been said, serves as a substitute for hereditary monarchy as a symbol and focus of nationalism.[69] The document soon became hedged with divinity in a young republic of disparate states in need of union. Today, the doctrines of 'Constitutional Originalism' and 'Strict Constructionism' have an extraordinary, quasi-religious appeal to many Americans, not least to a priesthood of lawyers who are the keepers and interpreters of the sacred text. But can they be called democrats when they are defending the rectitude of a pre-democratic document ratified by members of the conventions of the original thirteen states, which excluded the majority of the population from the vote?[70] Still, constitutional correctness has become central to contemporary political and legal debate, a fixation that seems rather fanciful to the British, who, given their own traditions, are wary of political documents with historic claims to inviolability.

It may seem surprising that Americans, who vote on virtually everything from gay marriage to marijuana use, have never had an opportunity to reconsider their eighteenth-century Constitution in a referendum. The comparison with Britain, which reshapes its more elastic Constitution with relative ease, is suggestive. The great paradox of America is its simultaneous belief in the future and its veneration of the past. There is a weightlessness of life in a nation that both dreads and is drawn to change, committed to the future but uncertain what the future might bring. Americans have sanctified a Constitution built, as Bryce put it, for 'safety' not for 'action'.[71] It recalls a less complicated past, providing consoling ballast in times of uncertainty. But as the reactionary Maine discerned and desired, it has been an obstruction to change. An impatient, pragmatic people have subdued a continent, but their system of government has been slow to adapt to shifting conditions and has consequently failed to provide political contentment.

It has been said that myth making, indifference to history, and selective memory have impaired the American commitment to democracy.[72] An unthinking 'cult of the Constitution' has left the United States immobilized at important moments in its history, a point made by Bagehot and other commentators in the nineteenth century, who observed that blind veneration of the Constitution prevented Americans from improving their government.[73] In a politics troubled by factionalism and partisanship, human failings dreaded by the founders, Americans have evaded the constitutional constraints on reform less by amendment than through the courts—and by stealth. It is worth recalling that when it has suited them most of the more memorable US Presidents, including Jackson, Lincoln, and Franklin Roosevelt, disregarded the 'limited clauses of an old state-paper' that they professed to revere. For no American politician has the courage to say of the Constitution, as it is said of kings, 'the King is dead, long live the King'.

Notes

CHAPTER I

1. For a study of the civil religion of the US Constitution see Sanford Levinson, *Constitutional Faith* (Princeton, 1988).
2. See www.govtrack.us/congress/record.
3. *New York Times*, 23 May 2009, A11.
4. *The Federalist*, no. 10.
5. www.access.gpo.gov/congress.senate/farewell.
6. *The Times*, 22 May 1788.
7. Quoted, Gordon Wood, *Empire of Liberty: A History of the Early Republic, 1789–1815* (Oxford, 2009), 36–7.
8. Quoted in Michael Kammen, *The Machine that Would Go of Itself: The Constitution in American Culture* (New York, 1997), 22.
9. On this point see Robert A. Dahl, *How Democratic is the American Constitution?* (New Haven, Conn., and London, 2003).
10. Brendan McConville, *The King's Three Faces: The Rise and Fall of Royal America, 1688–1776* (Chapel Hill, NC, 2006), 63–70.
11. Sir Henry Sumner Maine, *Popular Government* (London, 1885), 51. See e.g. *Springfield Republican*, 21 Mar. 1886.
12. Frank Prochaska, *The Eagle and the Crown: Americans and the British Monarchy* (New Haven, Conn., and London, 2008), 19.
13. See Kammen, *The Machine that Would Go of Itself*, 46.
14. www.access.gpo.gov/congress.senate/farewell.
15. George Ticknor Curtis, *History of the Origin, Formation, and Adoption of the Constitution of the United States*, 2 vols. (London, 1854), i, p. xi.
16. www.access.gpo.gov/congress.senate/farewell.
17. Wood, *Empire of Liberty*, 42.
18. Quoted, ibid. 47.
19. Kammen, *The Machine that Would Go of Itself*, p. xx.
20. Edmund S. Morgan, *The Birth of the Republic 1763–1789* (Chicago, 1992), 146.
21. For a stimulating discussion of collective sovereignty and its constitutional implications see Christian Fritz, *American Sovereigns: The People and America's Constitutional Tradition Before the Civil War* (Cambridge, 2008).
22. D. W. Brogan, *The American Political System* (London, 1933), 15.
23. Charles Beard, *An Economic Interpretation of the Constitution of the United States* (New York, 1913), 10.

24. One of the best 19th-cent. studies is George Ticknor Curtis, *Constitutional History of the United States from their Declaration of Independence to the close of the Civil War*, 2 vols. (New York, 1896–7). For a recent comprehensive treatment see Akhil Reed Amar, *America's Constitution: A Biography* (New York, 2005). Neither Curtis nor Reed mentions any of the British commentators on the American Constitution.
25. Amar, *America's Constitution: A Biography*, 465; Finer, Bogdanor, and Rudden, *Comparing Constitutions* (Oxford, 1995), 1.
26. Arthur H. Shaffer, *The Politics of History: Writing the History of the American Revolution 1783–1815* (Chicago, 1975), 49, 143.
27. See Harvey Wish, *The American Historian: A Social-Intellectual History of the Writing of the American Past* (New York, 1960).
28. George Bancroft, *History of the Formation of the Constitution of the United States of America*, 2 vols. (New York, 1882), i. 3.
29. Morgan, *Birth of the Republic*, 146.
30. Kammen, *A Machine that Would Go of Itself*, 97.
31. Amar, *America's Constitution: A Biography*, 20–1.
32. Albert Shaw, 'Our Working Constitution', *The Dial*, 5 (Mar. 1885).
33. John Stuart Mill, 'M. de Tocqueville in America', *Edinburgh Review* (1840), *Collected Works of John Stuart Mill*, ed. John M. Robson, 33 vols. (Toronto, 1963–91), xviii. 182.
34. 'The Perpetuation of our Political Institutions', *Collected Works of Abraham Lincoln*, 8 vols. (Ann Arbor, 1953), i. 108–15.
35. William Hickey, *The Constitution of the United States* (Washington, DC, 1846), p. xvii.
36. Shaw, 'Our Working Constitution'.
37. James Kent, *Commentaries on American Law*, 4 vols. (New York, 1826–30), i. 200, 218, 220, 232–3.
38. Joseph Story, *Commentaries on the Constitution of the United States,* 3 vols. (Boston, Mass., 1833), i. 2, 715, 718.
39. Ibid.
40. *Niles' Weekly Register*, 18 Oct. 1834.
41. Basil Hall, *Travels in North America*, 2 vols. (Philadelphia, 1829), i. 239.
42. Alexis de Tocqueville, *Democracy in America*, ed. Harvey C. Mansfield and Delba Winthrop (Chicago, 2000), 585.
43. *John Stuart Mill on Politics and Society*, ed. Geraint L. Williams (Brighton, 1976), 213.
44. Ibid. 242, 246.
45. George Bancroft, *The History of the United States: From the Discovery of the American Continent,* 10 vols. (Boston, Mass., 1864–75), viii. 474.
46. See Robert J. Spitzer, 'The President's Veto Power', *Inventing the American Presidency*, ed. Thomas E. Cronin (Lawrence, Kan., 1989), 157–8, 173.
47. Prochaska, *The Eagle and the Crown*, ch. 1. See also Gordon Wood, *Revolutionary Characters: What Made the Founders Different* (New York, 2006), 52–3.

48. George Tickner Curtis, *Constitutional History of the United States, from the Declaration of Independence to the close of the Civil War*, 2 vols. (New York, 1889), i. 264.
49. See e.g. Allan Nevins and Henry Steele Commager, *America:The Story of a Free People* (Oxford, 1966), 125–6, which argues that the American Bill of Rights differed fundamentally from the historic English bills of rights of 1628 and 1689.
50. See E. Neville Williams, *The Eighteenth Century Constitution 1688–1815: Documents and Commentary* (Cambridge, 1970), 26–9.
51. Orestes Brownson, *The American Republic: Its Constitution, Tendencies and Destiny* (Wilmington, Del., 2003), 159.
52. See Godfrey Hodgson, *The Myth of American Exceptionalism* (New Haven, Conn., and London, 2009).
53. Thomas Paine, *Rights of Man, Common Sense, and Other Political Writings*, ed. Mark Philp (Oxford 1995), 238, 244.
54. Ibid. 238, 245.
55. *Boswell's Life of Johnson*, ed. George Birkbeck Hill, 6 vols. (Oxford, 1934), iii. 201.
56. David Paul Crook, *American Democracy in English Politics 1815–1850* (Oxford, 1965), 1; John Sainsbury, *Disaffected Patriots: London Supporters of Revolutionary America 1769–1782* (Kingston and Montreal, 1987), 164.
57. See Frank Thistlethwaite, *The Anglo-American Connection in the Early Nineteenth Century* (Philadelphia, 1959), ch. 2.
58. Edward Dicey, *Six Months in the Federal States* (London and Cambridge, 1863), 117.
59. Frank Prochaska, *The Republic of Britain 1760–2000* (London, 2000), 17–18.
60. On this issue see Kirsty Carpenter, *Refugees of the French Revolution: Émigrés in London, 1789–1802* (London, 1999).
61. *The Parliamentary History of England, from the Earliest Period to theYear 1803* (London, 1806–20), xxix, cols. 365–6; Jack N. Rakove, 'Why American Constitutionalism Worked', in Edmund Burke, *Reflections on the Revolution in France*, ed. Frank M.Turner (New Haven and London, 2003), 251–2.
62. Henry Hyndman, *The Coming Revolution in England* (London, 1884), 9. Sir Henry Maine discussed the unhappy effects of the French Revolution in *Popular Government* (1885).
63. Prochaska, *The Republic of Britain 1760–2000*, 23.
64. H. C. Allen, *Great Britain and the United States: A History of Anglo-American Relations (1783–1952)* (NewYork, 1955), 307–56.
65. See e.g. John T. Morse, *John Quincy Adams* (Boston, 1898), 141.
66. *Parliamentary Debates*, xxxiv (6 June 1816), cols. 1002–3.
67. *Edinburgh Review*, 33/65 (Jan. 1820), 80.
68. Jane Louise Mesick, *The English Traveller in America, 1785–1835* (NewYork, 1922), 322–3.

69. Beckles Wilson, *America's Ambassadors to England (1785–1928)* (New York, 1928), p. viii.
70. See e.g. James Bryce, 'The Historical Aspect of Democracy', *Essays on Reform* (London, 1867), 263.
71. See Prochaska, *The Eagle and the Crown*, ch. 2.
72. *The Diary of George Templeton Strong: The Civil War 1860–1865*, ed. Allan Nevins and Milton Halsey Thomas (New York, 1952), 52.
73. On the varieties of republicanism see Prochaska, *The Republic of Britain 1760–2000*.
74. Prochaska, *The Eagle and the Crown*, 23, *passim*.
75. *London Review*, 2/4 (Jan. 1936), 373–4.
76. Mill to Harriet Mill, 11 June 1855, *Collected Works of John Stuart Mill*, ed. Francis E. Mineka and Dwight N. Lindley (Toronto, 1972), xiv. 486.
77. Frances Trollope, *Domestic Manners of the Americans* (New York, 1949), 404.
78. Anthony Trollope, *North America*, 2 vols. (Philadelphia, 1862), ii. 310–11, 322.
79. Christopher Flynn, 'Coleridge's American Dream: Natural Language, National Genius and the Sonnets of 1794–5', *European Romantic Review*, 13 (Jan. 2002), 411.
80. *Specimens of the Table Talk of S. T. Coleridge*, 2 vols. (New York, 1835), ii. 79.
81. Charles Dickens, *American Notes* (Gloucester, Mass., 1968), 277–86.
82. Thomas Carlyle, 'The Present Time', *Latter-Day Pamphlets* (London, 1850), 23.
83. A list of these can be found in an appendix in Crook, *American Democracy in English Politics 1815–1850*.
84. Ibid. 21.
85. Chilton Williamson, 'Bentham Looks at America', *Political Science Quarterly*, 70 (Dec. 1955), 548.
86. *The Works of Jeremy Bentham*, ed. J. Bowring, 11 vols. (London, 1838–43), x. 63.
87. Ibid. iii. 446–7.
88. Crook, *American Democracy in English Politics 1815–1850*, 11–12.
89. Jeremy Bentham, *A Comment on the Commentaries and A Fragment on Government* (London, 1977), 502–3.
90. On various shades of opinion on America in these years see Crook, *American Democracy in English Politics 1815–1850*, 117.
91. Quoted ibid. 116.
92. R. K. Webb, *Harriet Martineau: A Radical Victorian* (New York, 1960), 134.
93. C. Vann Woodward, *The Old World's New World* (New York, 1991), p. xvi. See also Allan Nevins, *America through British Eyes* (New York, 1948); Kathleen Burk, *Old World, New World: Great Britain and America from the Beginning* (New York, 2007), 277–307.
94. For a recent study see *Harriet Martineau: Authorship, Society and Empire*, ed. Ella Dzelzainis and Cora Kaplan (Manchester, 2010).
95. Harriet Martineau, *Society in America*, 3 vols. (London, 1837), iii. 6, 23, 299.
96. Webb, *Harriet Martineau: A Radical Victorian*, 164, 168.
97. Quoted ibid. 158.

NOTES 147

98. Martineau, *Society in America*, i. 39, iii. 300. The sequel, *Retrospect of Western Travel* (1838) was more to their liking.
99. Martineau, *Society in America*, i. 1, 55, 74.
100. Prochaska, *The Eagle and the Crown*, 52–3.
101. Quoted in Valerie K. Pichanick, *Harriet Martineau: The Woman and her Work, 1802–76* (Ann Arbor, 1980), 239.
102. See Prochaska, *The Republic of Britain 1760–2000*, chs. 1–2.
103. Ibid.

CHAPTER 2

1. *Democracy in America* was first published in French in 4 vols., the first two in 1835 and the second two in 1840. It became customary to refer to the parts published in 1835 as vol. i and those published in 1840 as vol. ii.
2. *Tait's Edinburgh Magazine* (Aug. 1840).
3. *The Foreign Quarterly Review*, 15 (July 1835).
4. *Quarterly Review*, 57 (Sept. 1836), 134.
5. See e.g. *The American Monthly Magazine*, 12 (Oct. 1838).
6. *Quarterly Review*, 57 (Sept. 1836), 133.
7. Ibid. 134.
8. See John Stuart Mill, 'State of Society in America', *London Review*, 2 (Jan. 1836), 367.
9. See e.g. 'Democracy in America', *Blackwoods Edinburgh Magazine*, 37 (May 1835), 758–66. David Paul Crook, *American Democracy in English Politics 1815–1850* (Oxford, 1965), 199.
10. John Stuart Mill, 'M. de Tocqueville on Democracy in America', *Edinburgh Review* (1840), *Collected Works of John Stuart Mill*, ed. John M. Robson, 33 vols. (Toronto, 1963–91), xviii. 155–6.
11. Ibid. 156.
12. John Stuart Mill, 'De Tocqueville on Democracy in America', *London Review*, 2/3 (July 1835), 86.
13. Mill, 'M. de Tocqueville on Democracy in America', *Collected Works*, xviii. 156.
14. Mill, 'De Tocqueville on Democracy in America', *London Review*, 94.
15. Mill, 'M. de Tocqueville on Democracy in America', *Collected Works*, xviii. 156–7.
16. Ibid. 191–2.
17. Ibid. 192–3.
18. Mill, 'State of Society in America', 371.
19. Mill, 'M. de Tocqueville on Democracy in America', *Collected Works*, xviii. 171.
20. *John Stuart Mill on Politics and Society*, ed. Geraint L. Williams (Brighton, 1976), 113.
21. Mill, 'De Tocqueville on Democracy in America', *London Review*, 97.

22. Ibid. 95.
23. Alexis de Tocqueville, *Democracy in America*, ed. Harvey C. Mansfield and Delba Winthrop (Chicago, 2000), 57.
24. Mill, 'De Tocqueville on Democracy in America', *London Review*, 95–100.
25. Ibid. 102–3.
26. Ibid. 103.
27. Ibid. 104.
28. Ibid.
29. John Stuart Mill, *Considerations on Representative Government* (London, 1861), 254, 257.
30. Mill, 'De Tocqueville on Democracy in America', *London Review*, 106.
31. Ibid. 112.
32. Mill, 'M. de Tocqueville on Democracy in America', *Collected Works*, xviii. 174.
33. Ibid. 175; see also Mill, 'De Tocqueville on Democracy in America', *London Review*, 114.
34. Tocqueville, *Democracy in America*, 662.
35. Mill, 'M. de Tocqueville on Democracy in America', *Collected Works*, xviii. 176.
36. Ibid. 176–7.
37. Ibid. 177.
38. Ibid.
39. Mill, 'De Tocqueville on Democracy in America', *London Review*, 92.
40. Ibid.
41. Mill, 'State of Society in America', *London Review*, 378.
42. Ibid. 384–5.
43. Tocqueville, *Democracy in America*, 565.
44. Mill, 'De Tocqueville on Democracy in America, 92.
45. 'The Perpetuation of our Political Institutions', *Collected Works of Abraham Lincoln*, 8 vols. (Ann Arbor, 1953), i. 108–15.
46. Mill, 'M. de Tocqueville on Democracy in America', *Collected Works*, xviii. 177.
47. Albert William Levi, 'The Value of Freedom: Mill's Liberty (1859–1959)', *Ethics*, 70 (1959), 37.
48. Mill, 'M. de Tocqueville on Democracy in America', *Collected Works*, xviii. 178.
49. Ibid.
50. Mill's personal library, presented to Somerville College, Oxford, by Miss Helen Taylor in 1905, does not e.g. contain the constitutional writings of James Kent and Joseph Story, though it does contain a copy of John C. Calhoun's *A Disquisition on Government* (1851), presented to Mill by the Legislature of South Carolina.
51. John Stuart Mill, *On Liberty*, ed. David Spitz (New York, 1975), 62.
52. Mill, 'M. de Tocqueville on Democracy in America', *Collected Works*, xviii. 178.
53. Tocqueville, *Democracy in America*, 663.

54. Mill, 'The Californian Constitution', *Collected Works*, xxv. 1148.
55. Mill, 'State of Society in America', *London Review* (1836), 372.
56. Mill, 'M. de Tocqueville on Democracy in America', *Collected Works*, xviii. 200.
57. Ibid. 199–200.
58. Mill, 'State of Society in America', *London Review*, 371.
59. Mill, 'De Tocqueville on Democracy in America', *London Review*, 123.
60. Mill, *Considerations on Representative Government*, 30.
61. On this issue see Stefan Collini, *Absent Minds: Intellectuals in Britain* (Oxford, 2006), ch. 10.
62. Samuel Taylor Coleridge, *Specimens of Table Talk*, 2 vols. (New York, 1835), i. 109.
63. Mill to Theodore Gomperz, 17 Sept. 1862; Mill to John Lothrop Motley, 17 Sept. 1862, *Collected Works*, xv. 795–7.
64. Edward Dicey, *Six Months in the Federal States* (London and Cambridge, 1863), 126–7.
65. Henry Adams, *The Education of Henry Adams: An Autobiography* (Boston, Mass., and New York, 1918), 19.
66. Quoted in Howard Temperley, *Britain and America since Independence* (Basingstoke and New York, 2002), 45.
67. J. B. McMaster, *A History of the People of the United States, from the Revolution to the Civil War*, 8 vols. (New York, 1903), v. 287.
68. Mill, 'State of Society in America', *London Review*, 372.
69. Mill, 'De Tocqueville on Democracy in America', *London Review*, 122.
70. Ibid.
71. Thomas Carlyle, 'The Present Time', *Latter-Day Pamphlets* (London, 1850), 25.
72. Mill, 'De Tocqueville on Democracy in America', 124.
73. On this issue see Maurice Cowling, *Mill and Liberty* (Cambridge, 1963).
74. Lincoln, 'The Perpetuation of our Political Institutions, 114–15.
75. Mill, *On Liberty*, 106.
76. John M. Robson, *The Improvement of Mankind: The Social and Political Thought of John Stuart Mill* (Toronto, 1968), 106.
77. John Stuart Mill, *Autobiography* (London, 1873), 134.
78. Mill to Sarah Austin, 11 Mar. 1842, *Collected Works*, xiii. 506.
79. *Daily News*, 2 Jan. 1850, *Collected Works*, xxv. 1147–51.
80. Richard Reeves, *John Stuart Mill: Victorian Firebrand* (London, 2007), 263.
81. Mill, *Considerations on Representative Government*, 136.
82. Ibid. 157.
83. Ibid. 137–8.
84. Ibid. 146.
85. Ibid. 174.
86. Leslie Butler, *Critical Americans: Victorian Intellectuals and Transatlantic Liberal Reform* (Chapel Hill, NC, 2007), 116.
87. For an analysis of Mill's religion see Alan Millar, 'Mill on Religion', *The Cambridge Companion to Mill*, ed. John Skorupski (Cambridge, 1998), 176–202.

88. Larry Siedentop, *Tocqueville* (Oxford, 1993), 111–12.
89. Tocqueville, *Democracy in America*, 520.
90. Walter Bagehot, 'Principles of Political Economy', *Prospective Review*, 16 (Oct. 1848), 463.
91. For a discussion of Mill, Thomas Hare, and proportional representation see Jenifer Hart, *Proportional Representation: Critics of the British Electoral System 1820–1945* (Oxford, 1992), ch. 2.
92. *Considerations on Representative Government*, 146.
93. Ibid. 145–6, 152.
94. Ibid. 248–9.
95. Ibid. 250.
96. Ibid. 248–51.
97. Ibid. 251–2.
98. Ibid. 252–3.
99. Ibid. 307.
100. Ibid. 308.
101. Ibid. 304–5.
102. Ibid. 305.
103. Mill to Parke Godwin, 15 May 1865, *Collected Works*, xvi. 1052.
104. Mill 'The Contest for America', *Collected Works*, xxi. 142.
105. Reeves, *John Stuart Mill*, 334.
106. Mill to John Lothrop Motley, 31 Oct. 1862, *Collected Works*, xv. 800. President Lincoln issued his intention to free the slaves in Sept. 1862; the Emancipation Proclamation on 1 Jan. 1863.
107. Butler, *Critical Americans*, 79–80.
108. Lincoln 'The Perpetuation of our Political Institutions', 113–15.
109. Mill to John Elliot Cairnes, 26 Dec. 1863, *Collected Works*, xv. 911.
110. Mill to Peter Alfred Taylor, 28 May 1869, *Collected Works*, xvii. 1608.
111. *Godey's Lady's Book and Magazine* (July 1862), 65.
112. Mill to John Lothrop Motley, 26 Jan. 1863, *Collected Works*, xv. 826–7.
113. Mill to Edwin Godkin, 24 May 1865, *Collected Works*, xvi. 1055.
114. Mill to John Plummer, 1 May 1865, *Collected Works*, xvi. 1038–9.
115. Mill to John Elliot Cairnes, 28 May 1865, *Collected Works*, xvi. 10–57.
116. Mill to Roland G. Hazard, 7 June 1865, *Collected Works*, xvi. 1066.
117. Mill to Roland G. Hazard, 15 Nov. 1865, *Collected Works*, xvi. 1118.
118. Mill to Samuel Wood, 2 June 1867, *Collected Works*, xvi. 1278.
119. Mill to Henry Villard, 19 Jan. 1869, *Collected Works*, xvii. 1550.

CHAPTER 3

1. G. M. Young, 'The Greatest Victorian', *Today and Yesterday* (London, 1948), 237–43. See also Hugh Brogan, 'America and Walter Bagehot', *American Studies* (1977), xi, 3, 335–56. For a highly critical study of Bagehot see C. H. Sisson, *The Case of Walter Bagehot* (London, 1972).

2. *The Collected Works of Walter Bagehot*, ed. Norman St John-Stevas, 15 vols. (London, 1968–86), iii. 25.
3. Stefan Collini, Donald Winch, and John Burrow, *That Noble Science of Politics: A Study in Nineteenth-Century Intellectual History* (Cambridge, 1983), 173.
4. William Irvine, *Walter Bagehot* (London, 1939), 281–2.
5. Bagehot, *Collected Works*, vi. 99.
6. *The Economist* (25 Sept. 1937).
7. Leslie Stephen 'Walter Bagehot', *Studies of a Biographer*, 4 vols. (London, 1902), iii. 163.
8. Bagehot, *Collected Works*, iv. 283.
9. Ibid. 344–5.
10. He wrote in an essay on Gladstone that 'Lancashire is sometimes called "America and water:" we suspect it is America and very little water'. Walter Bagehot, *Biographical Studies*, ed. Richard Holt Hutton (London, 1881), 89.
11. Bagehot, *Collected Works*, iv. 328.
12. Bagehot, *The English Constitution*, 17.
13. Earl of Balfour, 'Introduction', *The English Constitution* (London, 1928), pp. vii–viii.
14. Brian Harrison, *The Transformation of British Politics 1860–1995* (Oxford, 1996), 14.
15. Crane Brinton, *English Political Thought in the Nineteenth Century* (London, 1933), 182.
16. Bagehot, *Collected Works*, vi. 390. See also Harrison, *Transformation of British Politics 1860–1995*, 15.
17. Bagehot, *The English Constitution, Appendix on Reform*, 201.
18. His italics; quoted in Alastair Buchan, *The Spare Chancellor: The Life of Walter Bagehot* (London, 1959), 116.
19. Walter Bagehot, *Literary Studies*, ed. Richard Holt Hutton, 2 vols. (London, 1879), ii. 141.
20. John Bowle, *Politics and Opinion in the Nineteenth Century: An Historical Introduction* (New York, 1954), 259.
21. Quoted Brinton, *English Political Thought in the Nineteenth Century*, 182.
22. Quoted in Stephen, 'Walter Bagehot', *Studies of a Biographer*, iii. 184.
23. Buchan, *The Spare Chancellor: The Life of Walter Bagehot*, 64.
24. *Life, Letters and Journals of George Ticknor*, ed. George Stillman Hillard, 2 vols. (Boston, Mass., 1876), ii. 362–3.
25. Irvine, *Walter Bagehot*, 253, 282.
26. Bagehot, *The English Constitution*, 38.
27. Stephen, 'Walter Bagehot', *Studies of a Biographer*, iii. 177.
28. Bagehot, *The English Constitution*, 5.
29. Ibid. 23.
30. See e.g. James M. Beck, *The Constitution of the United States* (Oxford, 1922), 106.
31. Bagehot, *The English Constitution*, 158–9.

32. Viscount Bryce, *The Study of American History* (Cambridge, 1921), 25.
33. Bagehot, *The English Constitution*, 17–19, 22.
34. Ibid. 17, 23.
35. Jean-Jacques Rousseau, *Basic Political Writings* (Indianapolis and Cambridge, 1987), p. xi.
36. Bagehot, *The English Constitution*, 22–3.
37. *The Economist* (15 Dec. 1860); Buchan, *The Spare Chancellor: The Life of Walter Bagehot*, 155.
38. Bagehot, *The English Constitution*, 23.
39. Bagehot, *Collected Works*, iv. 180–1. *The Economist* (25 Apr. 1863).
40. Bagehot, *Collected Works*, iv. 277.
41. Ibid. 238.
42. Ibid.
43. Brinton, *English Political Thought in the Nineteenth Century*, 194.
44. Edward Dicey, *Six Months in the Federal States* (London and Cambridge, 1863), 131.
45. Bagehot, *Collected Works*, iv. 301.
46. Ibid. 287.
47. Ibid. 289–91.
48. Bagehot, *The English Constitution*, 157.
49. Bagehot, *Collected Works*, iv. 239.
50. Norman St John-Stevas, *Walter Bagehot: A Study of his Life and Thought together with a Selection from his Political Writings* (Bloomington, 1959), 115.
51. Bagehot, *The English Constitution*, 21–2.
52. *The Times*, 13 Nov. 1862.
53. Bagehot, *Collected Works*, iv. 297.
54. Ibid. 222–5.
55. Ibid. 284.
56. Ibid. 283.
57. St John-Stevas, *Walter Bagehot*, 116–17.
58. Collini, Winch, and Burrow, *That Noble Science of Politics*, 180.
59. Bagehot, *Collected Works*, iv. 271–3.
60. Ibid. 299.
61. Ibid. 272.
62. Ibid. 278.
63. Ibid. 279.
64. Ibid. 279–80.
65. On the spoils system, see D. W. Brogan, *The American Political System* (London, 1933), 183–204.
66. Bagehot, *Collected Works*, iv. 281.
67. Ibid.
68. Ibid. 279.
69. Bagehot, *The English Constitution*, 24.
70. Bagehot, *Collected Works*, iv. 369–71.

NOTES

71. Ibid. 371–3.
72. Ibid. 409.
73. Ibid. 407.
74. Ibid. 408.
75. Ibid. 408–9.
76. Ibid. 409.
77. Ibid. The view that Lincoln acted as a despot was not uncommon in Britain. See e.g. 'President Lincoln's Despotism', *The Examiner*, 16 Nov. 1861.
78. Bagehot, *The English Constitution*, 53.
79. See Arthur Schlesinger, Jr, *The Imperial Presidency* (Boston, Mass., 1973). Lord Hailsham famously described the office of Prime Minister as an 'elective dictatorship'. R. W. J. Hinton, 'The Prime Minister as an Elected Monarchy', *Parliamentary Affairs*, 13 (1959–60), 297–303.
80. Jacques Barzun, 'Bagehot as Historian', Bagehot, *Collected Works*, iii. 25.
81. Sissons, *The Case of Walter Bagehot*, 114.
82. Bagehot, *The English Constitution*, 48.
83. Louis J. Jennings, *Eighty Years of Republican Government in the United States* (New York, 1868), 36.
84. See Frank Prochaska, *The Eagle and The Crown: Americans and the British Monarchy* (New Haven, Conn., 2008), ch. 1.
85. John Adams, *A Defence of the Constitutions of Government of the United States of America*, 3 vols. (Philadelphia, 1797), i. 87, iii. 159.
86. Walter Bagehot, *Physics and Politics* (London, 1887), 53; Bagehot, *Literary Studies*, i, p. lv.
87. Bagehot, *The English Constitution*, 157.
88. Bagehot, *Collected Works*, iv. 223.
89. Bagehot, *The English Constitution*, 159–60.
90. Bagehot, *Collected Works*, iv. 192.
91. Ibid. 413.
92. Ibid. 418.
93. Ibid. 193.
94. Ibid. 420.
95. Ibid. 420–1.
96. *The Economist* (30 Sept. 1871).
97. Bagehot, *Collected Works*, iv. 425–7.
98. St John-Stevas, *Walter Bagehot*, 114.
99. Bagehot, *Collected Works*, iv. 410.
100. Ibid. 426.
101. Ibid.
102. Ibid. viii. 351–4.
103. Bagehot, *The English Constitution*, 160–1.
104. Ibid., introduction to the 2nd edn. (1872), 220–1.
105. Bagehot, *Collected Works*, viii. 363.

106. Ibid. 364–7.
107. Ibid.
108. *The Literary World*, 1 May 1873.
109. *The Works of Walter Bagehot*, 5 vols. (Hartford, 1891); Brogan, 'America and Walter Bagehot', 338.
110. Woodrow Wilson, 'A Literary Politician', *Atlantic Monthly* (Nov. 1895), 670.
111. Buchan, *The Spare Chancellor*, 157.

CHAPTER 4

1. *The Letters of Thomas Babington Macaulay*, ed. Thomas Pinney, 6 vols. (London, 1974–81), vi. 96.
2. For Maine's parentage and early life see George Feaver, *From Status to Contract: A Biography of Sir Henry Maine 1822–1888* (London, 1969), ch. 1. See also M. E. Grant Duff, *Sir Henry Maine: A Brief Memoir of his Life* (London, 1892).
3. Grant Duff, *Sir Henry Maine*, 9–10.
4. Feaver, *From Status to Contract*, 21. See also Stefan Collini, Donald Winch, and John Burrow, *That Noble Science of Politics: A Study in Nineteenth-Century Intellectual History* (Cambridge, 1983), 210.
5. Henry Maine, *Ancient Law* (New York, 1873), p. v.
6. Feaver, *From Status to Contract*, 43.
7. Norman St John-Stevas, *Walter Bagehot: A Study of his Life and Thought together with a Selection from his Political Writings* (Bloomington, 1959), 57–8. See the letter on *Physics and Politics* from Maine to Bagehot in Mrs Russell Barrington, *Life of Walter Bagehot* (London, 1914), 282.
8. A new edn. of Maine's *Popular Government* appeared in 1976 published by the Liberty Fund. See also the reappraisal of Maine's work in a book of essays titled *The Victorian Achievement of Sir Henry Maine*, ed. Alan Diamond (Cambridge, 1991).
9. Sir Henry Sumner Maine, *Popular Government* (Indianapolis, 1976; a reprint of the London edn. of 1885), 21–2.
10. Benjamin Evans Lippincott, *Victorian Critics of Democracy* (Minneapolis, 1938), 189.
11. Maine, *Popular Government* (3rd edn., London, 1886), 172–3.
12. Albert Venn Dicey, *Lectures on the Relation between Law and Public Opinion in England during the Nineteenth-Century* (London, 1962), 461.
13. Maine, *Popular Government* (1st edn. London, 1885), 174.
14. Ernest Barker, *Political Thought in England from Herbert Spencer to the Present Day* (New York and London, 1938), 167.
15. Ibid.
16. Ibid. 167–8.
17. *The Victorian Achievement of Sir Henry Maine*, 19.
18. Maine, *Popular Government*, 166.

19. Ibid. 182.
20. Ibid. 183–4.
21. Ibid. 102–4.
22. *New Princeton Review*, 3 (May 1886).
23. Maine, *Popular Government*, 104–5.
24. Crane Brinton, *English Political Thought in the Nineteenth Century* (London, 1933), 278.
25. Maine, *Popular Government*, 175.
26. Ibid. 105–8.
27. Like many of his generation he may have been influenced by Bagehot's *Physics and Politics*.
28. Ibid. 114–15.
29. Ibid. 102–8.
30. Brinton, *English Political Thought in the Nineteenth Century*, 278; William Graham, *English Political Philosophy from Hobbes to Maine* (New York 1971), 390–1.
31. Maine, *Popular Government*, 122.
32. *The Andover Review*, 5 (May 1886).
33. Maine, *Popular Government*, 145, 147.
34. Ibid. 149.
35. See e.g. *Proceedings of the American Academy of Arts and Sciences*, 23 (May 1887–May 1888), 356–66; *The Unitarian Review and Religious Magazine*, 25 (June 1886); *Andover Review*, 5 (May 1886).
36. *The Critic*, 6 March 1886.
37. *The Literary World*, 15 May 1886.
38. *Christian Union*, 22 Sept. 1887.
39. *The Notebooks of Matthew Arnold*, ed. H. F. Lowry, K. Young, and W. H. J. Dunn (Oxford, 1952), 409; K. Allott, *Five Uncollected Essays of Matthew Arnold* (Liverpool, 1953), 23–31.
40. Quoted, Feaver, *From Status to Contract*, 237.
41. John Morley, 'Sir Henry Maine on Popular Government', *Fortnightly Review*, 39 (1886), 153–73. This article was reprinted in *The Eclectic Magazine of Foreign Literature*, 43 (April 1886).
42. Grant Duff, *Sir Henry Maine*, 80.
43. Maine, *Popular Government*, 52. The maxim was adopted from Sir James Stephen, *Liberty, Fraternity, and Equality* (London, 1873), 239.
44. On Maine and imperialism see Karuna Mantena, *Alibis of Empire: Henry Maine and the Ends of Liberal Imperialism* (Princeton, 2010).
45. Feaver, *From Status to Contract*, 181.
46. Maine, *Popular Government*, 190.
47. Ibid. 199.
48. Frank Prochaska, *The Republic of Britain, 1760–2000* (London, 2000), 1.
49. Maine, *Popular Government*, 201.
50. Ibid. 209.

51. Ibid. 72–3.
52. Ibid. 80–1.
53. Ibid. 90–104.
54. Ibid. 86–7
55. Ibid. 87–8.
56. George Bancroft, *History of the Formation of the Constitution of the United States of America*, 2 vols. (New York, 1882), i. 3.
57. Maine, *Popular Government*, 247.
58. Ibid. 87–8.
59. Lippincott, *Victorian Critics of Democracy*, 178.
60. Maine, *Popular Government*, 26.
61. Ibid. 244.
62. Ibid. 26.
63. Ibid. 212.
64. J. Elliot, *Debates in the Several State Conventions, on the Adoption of the Federal Constitution*, 5 vols. (Philadelphia and Washington, DC, 1866), iii. 58–9.
65. http://memory.loc.gov/ammem/collections/continental/Randolph.
66. Prochaska, *Republic of Britain*, 19–25.
67. Richard N. Rosenfeld, *American Aurora* (New York, 1997), 477.
68. See Frank Prochaska, *The Eagle and the Crown: Americans and the British Monarch* (New Haven, Conn., and London, 2008), 53.
69. *Life and Speeches of Henry Clay*, ed. Daniel Mallory, 2 vols. (New York, 1844), ii. 378–9.
70. http://www.worldwideschool.org/library/books/hst/northamerican/UnitedStatesPresidentsinauguralSpeeches.
71. The observation first appeared in Goldwin Smith's *The Civil War in America* (London, 1866), but was widely cited elsewhere, including America. See e.g. *Prairie Farmer* (18 June 1870).
72. Maine, *Popular Government*, 214.
73. Ibid. 215–16.
74. Ibid. 215.
75. Ibid. 217–19.
76. Ibid. 222.
77. See e.g. *The Unitarian Review and Religious Magazine*, 25 (June 1886).
78. Maine, *Popular Government*, 182–4.
79. Ibid. 224–5.
80. http://www.senate.gov/legislative/common/briefing/Senate_legislative_process.
81. Maine, *Popular Government*, 227.
82. Ibid. 228.
83. Ibid. 229.
84. Ibid. 228.
85. Ibid. This is the *Federalist* essay in which Madison considered slaves as property not as persons.

86. Ibid. 236.
87. Ibid.
88. *The Unitarian Review and Religious Magazine*, 25 (June 1886).
89. Maine, *Popular Government*, 241.
90. Ibid. 242.
91. Ibid. 242–3.
92. Ibid. 243–4.
93. Ibid. 245–6.
94. Ibid. 246–7.
95. Ibid. 122–3.
96. Ibid. 247.
97. Peter Viereck, *Conservatism from John Adams to Churchill* (Princeton, 1956), 32.
98. *The Victorian Achievement of Sir Henry Maine*, 26–7.
99. John Bowle, *Politics and Opinion in the Nineteenth Century: An Historical Introduction* (New York, 1954), 257.
100. George A. Feaver, 'The Political Attitudes of Sir Henry Maine: Conscience of a 19th Century Conservative', *Journal of Politics*, 27/2 (May 1965), 290–317.
101. Barker, *Political Thought in England*, 169.
102. *The Critic*, 6 March 1886.
103. Brinton, *English Political Thought in the Nineteenth Century*, 271–2.
104. Maine, *Popular Government*, 51. See *Springfield Republican*, 21 Mar. 1886.
105. *The Baptist Quarterly Review*, 8 (July 1886).
106. Brinton, *English Political Thought in the Nineteenth Century*, 274.
107. Feaver, 'The Political Attitudes of Sir Henry Maine', 315.
108. *The Victorian Achievement of Sir Henry Maine*, 23–4.

CHAPTER 5

1. H. A. L. Fisher, *James Bryce*, 2 vols. (New York, 1927), i. 295.
2. Quoted ibid. 59–60.
3. For a recent biography of Bryce, see John T. Seaman, Jr, *A Citizen of the World: The Life of James Bryce* (London, 2006). For a survey of his American associations and travel, see Edmund Ions, *James Bryce and American Democracy 1870–1922* (London, 1968). For an analysis of *The American Commonwealth* half a century after its publication see *Bryce's 'American Commonwealth': Fiftieth Anniversary*, ed. Robert C. Brooks (New York, 1939). For an excellent analysis of the book more recently see Hugh Tulloch, *James Bryce's American Commonwealth: The Anglo-American Background* (Woodbridge, Suffolk, 1988).
4. Mrs Russell Barrington, *Life of Bagehot* (London, 1914), 33.
5. See Leslie Butler, *Critical Americans: Victorian Intellectuals and Transatlantic Liberal Reform* (Chapel Hill, NC, 2007).
6. Kathleen Burk, *Old World, New World: Great Britain and America from the Beginning* (New York, 2007), 297.

7. James Bryce, Speech at Pilgrim's Dinner, 23 Mar. 1907.
8. Stefan Collini, Donald Winch, and John Burrow, *That Noble Science of Politics: A Study in Nineteenth-Century Intellectual History* (Cambridge, 1983), 243.
9. James Bryce, *The American Commonwealth*, 2 vols. (2nd edn. London, 1889), i, pp. vii–ix.
10. Seaman, *Citizen of the World*, 147.
11. Collini, Winch, and Burrow, *That Noble Science of Politics*, 237.
12. Bryce, *The American Commonwealth*, i. 2, 5.
13. For a discussion of the seminar see Burton Bernard, *James Bryce: The American Commonwealth* (St Louis, 1990), 64–8.
14. Bryce, *The American Commonwealth*, i. 4.
15. Ibid.
16. Quoted, George Feaver, *From Status to Contract: A Biography of Sir Henry Maine 1822–1888* (London, 1969), 254.
17. Bryce, *The American Commonwealth*, i. 8.
18. For an early expression of Bryce's view on this issue see James Bryce. 'The Historical Aspect of Democracy', *Essays on Reform* (London, 1867), 251–78.
19. See Murney Gerlach, *British Liberalism and the United States: Political and Social Thought in the Late Victorian Age* (New York, 2001).
20. Tulloch, *James Bryce's American Commonwealth*, 2.
21. Ibid. 178.
22. Ions, *James Bryce and American Democracy 1870–1922*, 129–32.
23. Frederic Harrison, 'Mr Bryce's "American Commonwealth"', *The Eclectic Magazine of Foreign Literature* (Feb. 1889).
24. J. W. Burrow, 'Some British Views of the United States Constitution', in R. C. Simmons (ed.), *The United States Constitution: The First 200 Years* (Manchester, 1989), 128.
25. Lord Acton, 'The American Commonwealth', *English Historical Review*, 4/14 (Apr. 1889), 388–9.
26. *The Critic: a Weekly Review of Literature and the Arts,* 5 Jan. 1889.
27. For one of the more elaborate comparisons see *The Andover Review: A Religious and Theological Monthly*, 11 (May 1889).
28. See James Bryce, 'The Predictions of Hamilton and de Tocqueville', *Johns Hopkins Studies in Historical and Political Science*, 5th ser. 9 (1887), 5–57.
29. *Political Science Quarterly*, 4/1 (Mar. 1889), 153–69.
30. *Christian Union*, 21 Feb. 1889.
31. *New England and Yale Review*, 14 (June 1889).
32. Several reviewers made this point. See e.g. *Kansas City Star*, 28 May 1889; *The Chautauquan: A Weekly Magazine* (April 1889); *The Andover Review: A Religious and Theological Monthly*, 11 (May 1889).
33. Bryce, *The American Commonwealth*, i. 25.
34. Ibid. 25–6.

35. Ibid. 298.
36. Quoted in Michael Kammen, *Mystic Chords of Memory: The Transformation of Tradition in American Culture* (New York, 1991), 173–4.
37. Ions, *James Bryce and American Democracy 1870–1922*, 120.
38. Bryce, *The American Commonwealth*, ii. 229.
39. See Charles Ellis Stevens, *Sources of the Constitution of the United States, considered in relation to colonial and English history* (New York and London, 1894), which developed many of the points made by Bryce.
40. Ibid. i. 26, 32.
41. This point was well taken by Americans. See *New Englander and Yale Review*, 14 (June 1889).
42. Bryce, *The American Commonwealth*, i. 25.
43. Ibid. 582–3; H. A. Tulloch, 'Changing British Attitudes towards the United States in the 1880s', *Historical Journal*, 20/4 (1977), 827–8.
44. Charles Wentworth Dilke, *Greater Britain: A Record of Travel in English-Speaking Countries during 1866–7* (Philadelphia and London, 1869), pp. v, 268.
45. William Gladstone, 'Kin Beyond the Sea', *North American Review* (Sept./Oct. 1878).
46. For Bryce's views on the Venezuelan boundary dispute see Seaman, *Citizen of the World*, 176–8.
47. Quoted in Stuart Anderson, *Race and Rapprochement: Anglo-Saxonism and Anglo-American Relations, 1895–1904* (London and Toronto, 1981), 178.
48. Matthew Arnold, *Civilization in the United States* (New York, 1888), 72.
49. Peter Mandler, *The English National Character: The History of an Idea from Edmund Burke to Tony Blair* (New Haven, Conn., and London, 2006), 134.
50. Quoted in Seaman, *Citizen of the World*, 139.
51. James Bryce, *The Hindrances to Good Citizenship* (New Haven, Conn., 1909), 12.
52. Bryce, *The American Commonwealth*, i. 299–300.
53. Ibid. 300–4.
54. Ibid. 304.
55. Ibid. 36–7.
56. Ibid. 42.
57. Ibid. 41–2.
58. Henry Jones Ford, *The Rise and Growth of American Politics: A Sketch of Constitutional Development* (New York, 1898), 369.
59. Bryce, *The American Commonwealth*, i. 51.
60. Ibid. 289.
61. Tulloch, *James Bryce's American Commonwealth*, 63.
62. Bryce, *The American Commonwealth*, i. 73, 80.
63. Ibid. 80.
64. Ibid. ii. 200.
65. Ibid. i. 73–80.

66. Ibid. 75.
67. Ibid. 65–6.
68. Ibid. 60–1.
69. See William Edward Hartpole Lecky, *Democracy and Liberty*, 2 vols. (London and New York, 1896), i. 365.
70. Bryce, *The American Commonwealth*, i. 109–10, 120.
71. See *New York Times*, Op-Ed, 14 Jan. 2010.
72. Bryce, *The American Commonwealth*, i. 100. 120
73. On this issue see the *New York Times,* Op-Ed, 11 Jan. 2010.
74. Bryce, *The American Commonwealth*, i. 117–19.
75. Ibid. 118.
76. Ibid. 138–41.
77. Ibid. 143–4.
78. Ibid. 145–6.
79. Bryce, *The American Commonwealth*, i. 149.
80. *Political Science Quarterly*, 4/1 (Mar. 1889), 159. See also *Christian Union*, 39 (21 Feb. 1889).
81. Leslie Butler, *Critical Americans: Victorian Intellectuals and Transatlantic Liberal Reform* (Chapel Hill, NC, 2007), 217–18.
82. Bryce, *The American Commonwealth*, ii. 697.
83. Ibid. i. 638.
84. Ibid. 653.
85. Jane Louise Mesick, *The English Traveller in America 1785–1835* (New York, 1922), 323–4.
86. Ions, *James Bryce and American Democracy 1870–1922*, 137.
87. Bryce, *The American Commonwealth*, ii. 133.
88. Ibid. i. 76–7.
89. *The Critic: a Weekly Review of Literature and the Arts*, 11 (5 Jan. 1889).
90. Kammen, *Mystic Chords of Memory*, 121.
91. *Century Illustrated Magazine*, 37/5 (Mar. 1889).
92. *Christian Union*, 21 February 1889.
93. *The Critic: a Weekly Review of Literature and the Arts*, 11 (5 Jan. 1889).
94. Bryce, *The American Commonwealth*, ii. 225.
95. Ibid. 232–42.
96. On this issue see Tulloch, *James Bryce's American Commonwealth* , 146–7.
97. Collini, Winch, and Burrow, *That Noble Science of Politics*, 240.
98. Bryce, *The American Commonwealth*, ii. 243–54.
99. Ibid. 307–14.
100. Ibid. 313–14.
101. Ibid. See *The Andover Review*, 11 (May 1889).
102. Bryce, *The American Commonwealth,* ii. 404.
103. Ibid. 404–5.
104. Ibid. 408.
105. Ibid. 408–9.

106. Ibid. 409–10.
107. Ibid. 411.
108. Ibid. 411–23.
109. Ibid. 436–49.
110. Ibid. 450–60.
111. Ibid. 459.
112. Ibid. 460.
113. Ibid.
114. Ibid. 599–610.
115. Ibid. 702.
116. See James Bryce, 'The Essential Unity of England and America', *Atlantic Monthly*, 82 (1898), 22–9.
117. James Bryce, 'An Age of Discontent', *The Eclectic Magazine of Foreign Literature*, 53 (Feb. 1891).
118. Acton, 'The American Commonwealth', 392.

CHAPTER 6

1. James Bryce, *The American Commonwealth* (London, 1889), ii. 699.
2. www.teachingamericanhistory.org/convention/delegates.
3. On this issue see Charles Ellis Stevens, *Sources of the Constitution of the United States, considered in Relation to Colonial and English history* (New York and London, 1894). See also Bernard Bailyn, *Ideological Origins of the American Revolution* (Cambridge, Mass., 1967).
4. J. W. Burrow, 'Some British Views of the United States Constitution', in R. C. Simmons (ed.), *The United States Constitution: The First 200 Years* (Manchester, 1989), 132.
5. John Stuart Mill, *Considerations on Representative Government* (8th edn. London, 1861), 96–7.
6. A.V. Dicey, *Introduction to the Study of the Law of the Constitution* (London, 1915), 135.
7. William Edward Hartpole Lecky, *Democracy and Liberty*, 2 vols. (London and New York, 1896), i. 7–8.
8. For an example of the exceptionalist argument see George Tickner Curtis, *Constitutional History of the United States, from their Declaration of Independence to the close of the Civil War*, 2 vols. (New York, 1889), i. 264. See also Geoffrey Hodgson, *The Myth of American Exceptionalism* (New Haven, Conn., and London, 2009).
9. Woodrow Wilson, *Congressional Government: A Study in American Politics* (Boston, Mass., and New York, 1885), 307.
10. Stevens, *Sources of the Constitution of the United States considered in Relation to Colonial and English History*, viii–ix, xii.
11. Henry Jones Ford, *The Rise and Growth of American Politics: A Sketch of Constitutional Development* (New York, 1898), 72.

12. Charles Beard, *An Economic Interpretation of the Constitution of the United States* (New York, 1913), 2–3.
13. Stevens, *Sources of the Constitution of the United States considered in Relation to Colonial and English History*, x.
14. David Hackett Fischer, *Albion's Seed: Four British Folkways in America* (New York and Oxford, 1989), 47.
15. Edmund Ions, *James Bryce and American Democracy 1870–1922* (London, 1968), 135.
16. Harriet Beecher Stowe, *Sunny Memories of Foreign Lands*, 2 vols. (Boston, Mass., 1854), i. 18.
17. See e.g. Russell Kirk, *America's British Culture* (New Brunswick, NJ, 1993); Samuel Huntington, *Who are We? The Challenges to America's National Identity* (New York, 2004); See also, Frank Prochaska, *The Eagle and the Crown: Americans and the British Monarchy* (New Haven, Conn., and London, 2008), 200.
18. Royal Archives, VIC/M 65/63.
19. See Reginald Horsman, *Race and Manifest Destiny: The Origins of Racial Anglo-Saxonism* (Cambridge, Mass., and London, 1981).
20. Frederick William Chapman, 'The Changed Significance of "Anglo-Saxon"', *Education*, 21 (Feb. 1900), 367–9.
21. *Political Science Quarterly*, 4/1 (March 1889), 169.
22. *The Collected Works of Walter Bagehot*, ed. Norman St John-Stevas, 15 vols (London, 1968–86), iv. 328.
23. Sir Henry Maine, *Popular Government* (London, 1885), 41–2.
24. Quoted in Merle Curti, *The Growth of American Thought* (New York, 1943), 675.
25. Michael J. Sewell, 'Queen of Our Hearts', in Steven Ickingrill and Stephen Mills (eds), *Victorianism in the United States: Its Era and its Legacy* (Amsterdam, 1992), 211–12.
26. *Dallas Morning News*, 20 June 1887.
27. Prochaska, *The Eagle and the Crown,* chs. 3, 5.
28. *New York Times*, 22 June 1887.
29. Frances Anne Kemble, *Further Records. 1848–1883*, 2 vols. (London, 1890), ii. 240.
30. Charles S. Campbell, *The Transformation of American Foreign Relations 1865–1900* (New York, 1976), 335–6.
31. On the history of Anglo-Saxonism see Horsman, *Race and Manifest Destiny: The Origins of American Racial Anglo-Saxonism* (Cambridge, Mass., and London, 1981).
32. H. A. Tulloch, 'Changing British Attitudes towards the United States', *Historical Journal*, 20/4 (1977), 839–40.
33. G. R. Searle, *A New England? Peace and War 1886–1918* (Oxford, 2004), 12.
34. A.V. Dicey, 'A Common Citizenship for the English Race', *Contemporary Review*, 71 (Apr. 1897).

NOTES 163

35. Alexis de Tocqueville, *Democracy in America*, ed. Harvey C. Mansfield and Delba Winthrop (Chicago and London, 2000), 7.
36. Hugh Tulloch, *James Bryce's American Commonwealth: The Anglo-American Background* (Woodbridge, Suffolk, 1988), 61–7.
37. Ibid. 56.
38. The American Bar Association unveiled its Memorial at Runnymede in 1957 that called Magna Carta the symbol of 'Freedom under the Law'.
39. Leslie Stephen, 'On the Choice of Representatives by Popular Constituencies', *Essays on Reform* (London, 1867), 95.
40. Goldwin Smith, 'The Experience of the American Commonwealth', *Essays on Reform*, 221.
41. John Stuart Mill, 'De Tocqueville on Democracy in America', *London Review* (July 1835), 114–15.
42. Maine, *Popular Government*, 59–60.
43. Those were not his exact words but what has come down to us from his speech in Parliament. See Jonathan Parry, 'Robert Lowe, First Viscount Sherbrooke', *Oxford Dictionary of National Biography* (Oxford, 2004).
44. Tocqueville, *Democracy in America*, 127, 190.
45. For American views see Wilson, *Congressional Government*, 97–101, 186–7; Ford, *The Rise and Growth of American Politics*, ch. 23.
46. www.access.gpo.gov/congress.senate/farewell.
47. Henry Adams, *The Education of Henry Adams* (Boston, Mass., 1918), 7.
48. Maine, *Popular Government*, 117.
49. Lecky, *Democracy and Liberty*, i. 66.
50. Ibid.
51. Maine, *Popular Government*, 115–18.
52. Lecky, *Democracy and Liberty*, i. 64.
53. Bryce, *The American Commonwealth*, ii. 615–26.
54. For a reassessment of Mill's views on participatory democracy see Alex Zakaris, 'John Stuart Mill, Individuality, and Participatory Democracy', in Nadia Urbinati and Alex Zakaris (eds), *J. S. Mill's Political Thought: A Bicentennial Reassessment* (Cambridge, 2007), ch. 8.
55. See James Bryce, *The Hindrances to Good Citizenship* (New Haven, Conn., 1909); Edmund Ions, *James Bryce and American Democracy 1870–1922* (London, 1968), 324.
56. Mill, 'De Tocqueville on Democracy in America', 97.
57. John Stuart Mill, *Principles of Political Economy* (Harmondsworth, 1970), 312–13.
58. *The Federalist with Letters of 'Brutus'*, ed. Terence Ball (Cambridge, 2003), 443.
59. Quoted in Tulloch, *James Bryce's American Commonwealth*, 104.
60. Jean-Jacques Rousseau, *Basic Political Writings* (Indianapolis and Cambridge, 1987), 168.
61. Lecky, *Democracy and Liberty*, i. 93.
62. Ibid.

63. Tocqueville, *Democracy in America*, 426–8.
64. Lecky, *Democracy and Liberty*, 93, 97.
65. Ibid. 94.
66. *The Federalist with Letters of 'Brutus'*, xix.
67. www.access.gpo.gov/congress.senate/farewell.
68. Bryce, *The American Commonwealth*, i. 304.
69. Michael Kammen, *A Machine that Would Go of Itself: The Constitution in American Culture* (New York, 1997), 22.
70. Robert A. Dahl, *How Democratic is the American Constitution?* (New Haven, Conn., and London, 2003), 2.
71. Viscount Bryce, *The Study of American History* (Cambridge, 1921), 25.
72. See e.g. Michael Kammen, *Mystic Chords of Memory: The Transformation of Tradition in American Culture* (New York, 1991).
73. See Hermann E. von Holst, *The Constitution and Political History of the United States*, 8 vols. (Chicago, 1876–92), i, ch. 2.

Index

Acton, Lord 75, 80, 100, 121, 126
Adams, Henry 35, 111, 135
Adams, John, President 64, 82, 85, 86
Albert, Prince 127
Alison, Archibald 19
American Anti Slavery Society 7
American Constitution, passim
  Amendments 11, 42, 68, 71, 102, 133
  Articles 3, 51, 62, 64, 85, 89, 90, 93
  Bill of Rights 4, 11
  and democracy 18, 58, 140
  monarchical elements 3, 63–4, 85–6, 106
  origins 8, 10–11, 22, 124–6
  reverence for 1, 4–5, 8, 10, 12, 126, 141–2
  and slavery 7, 8, 44, 46, 102
  symbolism 3, 141
American education 36, 46, 101
American exceptionalism vi, 4, 15, 36, 126, 129
  see also Anglo-American exceptionalism
American parties/party system 38, 58, 78, 96, 108, 112–14, 134
American Republic, The 11
American Revolution 2, 3, 4, 6, 11, 12, 22, 30, 90, 102, 122, 126
American Social Science Association 46
Angell, James B. 98
Anglo-American exceptionalism vi, 129
Anglo-Saxon unity/Anglo-Saxonism 16, 49, 50, 68, 79, 83, 96, 97, 103–4, 116, 124, 125–30, 132

Anne, Queen 10
Anti-Federalists 2, 138
Aristotle 78
Arnold, Matthew 97, 103

Bagehot, Walter 21, 40, 47–71, 72, 73, 77, 81, 86, 88, 91, 94, 97, 105–9, 123, 125, 127, 131, 136, 138, 139
  American Constitution 51–4, 57, 58–9, 62, 64–5, 67–8, 69, 71, 124, 133, 142
  Civil War 52, 54, 56, 57, 60, 62, 63, 65, 66, 67, 68
  English Constitution, The 63, 65, 70, 86
  federal government 55, 65
  Physics and Politics 64, 73
  President/presidency 55–6, 60, 62, 133
  slavery 52, 57, 61, 66, 67, 129
  Supreme Court 56–7
Bancroft, George 9, 75, 84
Barzun, Jacques 63
Beard, Charles 6, 125
Belfast 97
Belknap, Jeremy 6
Bennington, Battle of 128
Bentham, Jeremy 18, 27, 76
Beveridge, Albert 128
Blackstone, William 103
Blackwood's 19
Boston 34, 35, 45
British Constitution 9, 11, 12, 14, 16, 24, 48, 51, 52, 54, 65, 72, 82–3, 85, 91, 121, 140, 141

Brownson, Orestes 11
'Brutus' 138
Bryce, James 21, 96–121, 123, 125, 127, 132, 135, 136, 137, 138
  American Commonwealth, The 98, 99, 100–4, 107, 109, 111–12, 115, 121, 128
  American Constitution 99, 102–3, 105–6, 108–110, 121, 124, 126, 130, 141, 142
  Civil War 97, 117
  Holy Roman Empire, The 97
  House of Representatives 109, 111
  parties/party system 108–9, 112–13, 134
  President/presidency 106–9, 133
  plutocracy 118, 120, 121
  public opinion 115–16
  Senate/Senators 109
  slavery 102, 129
  spoils 109
  on Tocqueville 99, 101, 102, 116–17
Buchanan, James, President 53, 58
Burke, Edmund 14, 48, 74, 94, 121, 129
Bush, George W., President 53, 69

Cairnes, John Elliot 45
Calhoun, John C. 11
California Constitution 37
Calvin, John 105
Cambridge University 73, 97
Carlyle, Thomas 17, 36, 44, 61, 132
Charles I, King 10
Churchill, Winston 53
Civil War 30, 42, 44, 46, 52, 56, 57, 59, 62, 63, 65, 66, 67, 68, 93, 114, 117, 127, 134
Clay, Henry 86
Cleveland, Grover, President 135
Coleridge, Samuel Taylor 17, 35
Columbia University 98
Commentaries on American Law 8
Commentaries on the United States Constitution 8
Comte, Auguste 20

Congress 42, 43, 54, 55, 60, 65, 88, 90, 109, 111
Congressional Government 70, 110, 125
Constitution, United States, see American Constitution
Constitutional Convention, Philadelphia 5, 123, 140
Contemporary Review 130
Coolidge, Calvin, President 1
Corrupt Practices Act (1883) 136
corruption 58, 113–15, 135–6, 139–40
  see also elections/electioneering
Cromwell, Oliver 107

Daily News 37
Dartmouth v. Woodward (1819) 92
Darwin, Charles 73
Declaration of Independence 5, 15, 18, 39, 44, 67
Defoe, Daniel 138
Democracy 111
Democracy and Liberty 124, 135, 139
Democracy in America 7, 18, 21, 23–5, 27, 37, 40, 50, 80, 123, 131
Democratic-Republican Party 14
Dicey, Albert Venn 35, 74, 96, 97, 98, 103, 112, 124, 130, 138
Dicey, Edward 35
Dickens, Charles 17
Dilke, Charles 104
Discourse on the Constitution and Government of the United States 11
Domestic Manners of the Americans 16
Dred Scott decision (1857) 43, 57, 93

Economic Interpretation of the Constitution of the United States, An 6
Economist, The 47, 48, 66, 68
Edinburgh Review 15, 17, 25
education, *see* American education
egalitarianism 121, 131
Eggleston, Edward 102
elections/electioneering 41, 58–9, 113–15, 134
  see also corruption

elective monarchy 64, 85, 86 87, 106
Electoral College 41, 59, 69, 87, 92
Eliot, Charles W. 97
Emancipation Proclamation 44, 61
Emerson, Ralph Waldo 35, 97
English Bill of Rights 9, 11, 102
English Constitution, *see* British Constitution
English County Franchise Bill 91
English Historical Review 100
Esprit des Lois 88
Evarts, William 128
exceptionalism, *see* American exceptionalism

factionalism 2, 134, 140, 142
Feaver, George 73
Federalist 2, 5, 33, 42, 82, 87, 88, 90, 131, 134, 135
Federalists 2
filibustering 110
Ford, Henry Jones 125
Founding Fathers 2, 5, 9, 19, 29, 33, 48, 55, 56, 102, 105, 112, 131, 132, 135, 137, 141
Franklin, Benjamin 117
Freeman, Edward A. 97, 104
French Revolution 13, 14, 22, 24, 75, 122

George III, King 3, 12, 16, 63, 82, 85, 95, 106, 128
Gladstone, William Ewart 80, 104
Glasgow University 97
Goodnow, Frank 98
Grant, Ulysses S., President 68, 107
Grey, Edward 104

Hall, Basil, Captain 9, 24
Hamilton, Alexander 5, 42, 55, 82, 85, 86–7, 112
Hare, Thomas 40, 50
Harrison, Frederick 100
Harrison, William Henry, President 86
Hayes, Rutherford B., President 69

History of the United States 9
Hobbes, Thomas 76, 94, 105
Holland, Henry Richard Vassall, 3rd Baron 15
Holland, Thomas Erskine 98
Holmes, Oliver Wendell 98
Holy Roman Empire 87
Hoover, Herbert, President 53
House of Commons 55, 89, 90, 110–11
House of Lords 76, 89, 123
House of Representatives/ Representatives 55–6, 89, 90, 93, 109–111

Illinois, Springfield 7
India 75, 80
Introduction to the Study of the Law of the Constitution 124

Jackson, Andrew, President 21, 38, 77, 101, 107, 135, 142
Jacksonian democracy 18, 58, 116–17
Jay, John 5, 42, 82
Jefferson, Thomas 14, 15, 89
Johnson, Andrew, President 67, 68
Johnson, Samuel 12, 87
Joseph II, Emperor 87

Kansas, 46
Kemble, Fanny 129
Kent, James 6, 8, 33

Lancashire 48, 54
Latin American republics 15
Lecky, William Edward Hartpole 122, 124, 135, 136, 139–40
Lincoln, Abraham, President 7–8, 33, 37, 41, 44–5, 54, 59, 60–3, 64, 107, 108, 109, 123, 127, 132, 133, 142
London Review 25
Longfellow, Henry Wadsworth 97
Low, Seth 98

Lowe, Robert 133
Lowell, Abbott Lawrence 3
Lowell, James Russell 97, 129
loyalists 13

Macaulay, Thomas Babington 72
Machiavelli 76
Madison, James, President 2, 5, 14, 15, 20, 42, 82, 87, 134
Magna Carta 9, 102
Maine, Sir Henry Sumner 3, 21, 72–95, 97, 99, 106, 109, 123, 125, 127, 131, 133, 135, 136, 137, 138, 140
    American Constitution 72, 74, 79–85, 89, 91–2, 93–5, 124
    Ancient Law 73, 74, 75, 76, 97
    British Constitution 72, 82–3, 85, 91, 93, 94
    Civil War 93
    India 75, 80
    parties/party system 78, 134–5
    Popular Government 73–4, 75, 76, 79, 80, 82, 94–5, 99, 109
    President/presidency 85, 87, 133
    slavery 93
    Supreme Court 87–8, 92
Marbury v. Madison (1803) 29
Marshall, John 6
Martineau, Harriet 19–21, 24
Marx, Karl 95
Mill, John Stuart 7, 9, 15, 18, 21, 25–46, 50, 57, 58, 61, 62, 66, 74, 77, 80, 81, 88, 108, 112, 116, 122, 123, 124, 125, 127, 129, 131, 133, 134, 136, 137, 139, 140
    Autobiography 37
    Considerations on Representative Government 37–9, 42, 45, 58, 134
    federal system 28, 43
    municipal government 28
    On Liberty 37
    President/presidency 40–2, 133
    Principles of Political Economy 137
    slavery 32, 43–6, 129
    Supreme Court 29, 43
    tyranny of the majority 31–2
    women's rights 32
    monarchy 9, 64, 82, 83–4, 85–6
    see also elective monarchy
Monroe, James, President 1, 15
Montana 97
Montesquieu 24, 26, 82, 88, 100, 103, 138
Morley, John 80
Motley, John Lothrop 44
Musset, Alfred de 23

Napoleonic Wars 14, 17, 75
National Review 49, 57
New England 28, 35, 45
New England town meeting 28, 103
New England and Yale Review 101
New Hampshire, Concord 9, 114
New York 31, 34, 89, 114, 128
Nineteenth Century 100
Northern Pacific Railway 97

Obama, Barack, President 1
Ohio 109, 114
'On a Certain Condescension in Foreigners' 129
Oxford University 97

Paine, Thomas 11, 12, 13, 15, 90, 117, 129
parties/party system, *see* American parties/party system
Pater, Walter 97
Philadelphia 31, 48, 132
Pierce, Franklin, President 107
plutocrats/plutocracy 118, 120, 121, 136
Poland 87
Polk, James K., President 107
Political Science Quarterly 101
Popular Government 3
President/presidency 40–2, 55, 56, 59–60, 62, 85–7, 106–9, 133

Quarterly Review 17, 24, 73

Ramsey, David 6
Reconstruction 46, 66
Reflections on the Revolution in France 14
Reform Act (1832) 19, 23, 27, 52, 122
Reform Act (1884) 81, 83
religion 33, 39–40
republicanism 13, 14–15, 21
Revolution of 1688 9
Rhode Island 89, 114
Rights of Man 11–12, 15
Rise and Growth of American Politics, The 125
Roosevelt, Franklin D., President 53, 142
Roosevelt, Theodore, President 98, 100
Rousseau, Jean-Jacques 53, 75–6, 103, 138
Runnymede 132
Rush, Benjamin 3

Scofield, C. I. 128
Senate/Senators 42–3, 76, 85, 89, 90, 92, 93, 109–110
Seward, William 64
Shaw, Albert 7, 8
Six Months in the Federal States 35
slavery 2, 8, 11, 12, 15, 21, 32, 43–4, 45, 46, 52, 57, 61, 66, 67, 93, 102, 129
Smith, Goldwin 86, 97, 112, 133
Smith, Sydney 1, 15
Social Contract 53, 75–6
Society in America 20–1
Socrates 45
Sources of the Constitution of the United States 125
Spain 127
Specimens of Table Talk 35
Spoils/spoils system 59, 77, 109, 134, 135, 139
'State of Society in America' 32
Stephen, Leslie 133
Stevens, Charles Ellis 125, 126
Stevenson, Andrew 15

Storey, Joseph 6, 8–9, 11, 33
Stowe, Harriet Beecher 126
Supreme Court 5–6, 29, 43, 56–7, 87–8, 92, 93

Taylor, Harriet 16, 80
Thackeray, William Makepeace 79
Tilden, Samuel 69
Times, The (London) 2, 53, 56
Tocqueville, Alexis de 7, 10, 18, 21, 23–8, 30–9, 45, 48, 51, 57, 70, 74, 77, 80, 83, 87, 97–8, 100–3, 112, 115, 123, 131, 134, 136, 139
Traveler's Insurance Company 70
Trollope, Anthony 17, 79
Trollope, Frances 16, 24
Twain, Mark 111
tyranny of the majority 31, 51, 77, 117, 136

United States Constitution, *see* American Constitution
University College, London 47
Utilitarians 27

Vatican 87
Venezuela 104
veto 9
Victoria, Queen 90, 96, 127, 128
Virginia 32

War of 1812 14, 126
Washington, George 1, 2, 4, 5, 15, 58, 85, 87, 89, 105, 106, 141
Ways and Means Committee 111
Webster, Daniel 1, 6, 9, 11
Weems, Mason Locke, 5
Westminster Review 17, 18, 20
White, Theodore 98
William V, Stadtholder 86
Wilson, James 51
Wilson, Woodrow, President 70, 71, 98. 101, 110, 125, 127
Winthrop, John 126
women's rights 21, 32, 101
Wood, Samuel 46